The "Ithaca" Chapter of Joyce's *Ulysses*

Studies in Modern Literature, No. 27

A. Walton Litz, General Series Editor

Consulting Editor for Titles on James Joyce
Professor of English
Princeton University

Other Titles in This Series

The "Ithaca" Chapter of Joyce's *Ulysses*

by
Richard E. Madtes

UMI RESEARCH PRESS
Ann Arbor, Michigan

Produced and distributed by
UMI Research Press
an imprint of
University Microfilms International
Ann Arbor, Michigan 48106

Library of Congress Cataloging in Publication Data

Madtes, Richard E.
    The "Ithaca" chapter of Joyce's *Ulysses.*

    (Studies in modern literature ; no. 27)
    Revision of thesis (Ph.D.)–Columbia University, 1961.
    Bibliography: p.
    Includes index.
    1. Joyce, James, 1882-1941. Ulysses. 2. Joyce, James,
1882-1941–Technique. I. Title. II. Series.

PR6019.O9U6824 1983   823'.912   83-9248
ISBN 0-8357-1460-8

for my wife and daughter

Contents

viii   Contents

Preface

The original version of this book was written nearly a quarter of a century ago. Anyone at all familiar with the "Joyce industry" can imagine my qualms, after those many years, at the task of making the results of my research relevant for today. Even so, I was surprised to find that much said then is still valid and significant now. I have, however, amended and revised the entire text to exclude the outmoded and to include, as much as possible, recent findings and critical views about Joyce, *Ulysses,* and Ithaca.

The critical liberalism of Professor William York Tindall, with whom I worked at Columbia University, was a valuable antidote to my own early tendency to try to make such and such mean so and so and nothing else — a tendency one should abandon quickly when approaching a writer like Joyce. Other people helped me locate and examine various manuscripts and other materials. I am especially grateful to Professor A. Walton Litz of Princeton, William H. McCarthy, Jr. of the Rosenbach Foundation, William A. Jackson of Harvard's Houghton Library, Herbert Cahoon of the Pierpont Morgan Library, and Mrs. David Hayman at the University of Texas. Many others in this country, Ireland, and England paused in their busy lives to assist my efforts. Fellow experts on the episodes of *Ulysses* — Norman Silverstein (Circe), Robert Hurley (Proteus), and James Card (Penelope) — shared problems and solutions with me.

Introduction

The Ithaca episode of *Ulysses* asks questions — no fewer than 309 of them. Let us begin with a couple of our own. What justification is there for a book-length study of one of the novel's eighteen episodes, and further, why should that one be Ithaca?

Anyone who reads Joyce from beginning to end cannot help realizing that, from the standpoint of technique, his prose falls into two divisions, with the Sirens episode of *Ulysses* marking the dividing point. With important exceptions, the prose of *Stephen Hero, Dubliners, A Portrait of the Artist, Exiles,* and the first ten episodes of *Ulysses* (up to the Sirens) is comparatively conventional. The most important exception, of course, is the stream of consciousness technique, a major experiment indeed, and there were also lesser departures from conventional prose style, such as the childlike babble of the opening paragraphs of *A Portrait,* the newspaper headlines of the Aeolus episode, or the literary imitations in Scylla and Charybdis. Nevertheless, in 1919 the Sirens episode brought a change. Language and style, always primary concerns with Joyce, now became obsessions. Experiment and innovation became the rule. Every one of the last eight episodes of *Ulysses* is an adventure in technical virtuosity, as the artist who stated that he could do anything with words put himself to the test. The jumble of broken phrases which begins the Sirens episode may be regarded as Joyce's emphatic declaration of independence from linguistic convention. Here, in all actuality, is the inception of *Finnegans Wake.*

The first ten episodes of *Ulysses,* compared with the last eight, are short and relatively uncomplicated (relatively, for nothing in the book is simple). Together they account for only one third of the novel. And although they certainly deserve careful critical analysis and interpretation, few of them could justify a book-length study. The later episodes, though, are of a length and complexity that not merely justify but positively require extensive analysis. Their involved structures and intricate technical effects not only invite study as they stand in their present form, but also drive the student to search behind the scenes, so to speak, in an effort to discover the means and methods from which such compositions have evolved. For full understanding and appreciation, study of the text of one of these episodes "as is" is not enough; one must also examine the text in the process of becoming, and this means investigation of Joyce's voluminous notes, manuscripts, typescripts, and proofs.

This sort of comprehensive study, then, is attempted here with the seventeenth chapter of *Ulysses* — the seventy-two page "question-and-answer" episode in which Leopold Bloom, at about two o'clock in the morning of June 17, 1904, returns home accompanied by his "wonderful friend," as Joyce's notes refer to Stephen Dedalus. But why, from among the later episodes of the book, should Ithaca be singled out for this attention? The most important reason is that this episode contains the culmination of the events and emotions of the preceding day. This has not always been understood. The frequent nomination of the Circe episode as the novel's climax derives more from the popular personality of the candidate than from actual qualifications. With its swirling color, parades of people, and kaleidoscopic animation, Circe presents a marvelously entertaining show. Add to this the facts that it concludes the "Odyssey" proper and that it offers the significant scene in which Stephen smashes the brothel chandelier to the accompaniment of time's "livid final flame" and the "ruin of all space," and one can readily understand why Circe appears to be climactic. And indeed, judged by action and technique, it is climactic — nothing in the book comes close to its brilliant motion and stunning artistic effects. But to regard Circe, therefore, as *the* climax of *Ulysses* is to substitute energy and originality for ultimate significance. Stephen's destruction of the lamp may be the climax of Circe, but not of *Ulysses* — and a good thing, too, for otherwise we would face nearly 170 pages of anticlimax in the last three episodes.

Recent critics have seen this more clearly than the earlier ones. A. Walton Litz, for example, states unequivocally that "both the action and the stylistic development of *Ulysses* reach a climax in 'Ithaca.'"[1] The essence of the novel is the meeting of Bloom and Stephen and Bloom's return to home and Molly. Although the two men are together in the maternity hospital and the Nighttown brothel, they speak no more than a few words to each other; the actual meeting begins in the cabman's shelter and culminates in Bloom's kitchen and garden. The true climax of *Ulysses* appears in the mystical union which, in spite of their differences, Bloom and Stephen experience, followed by Bloom's achievement of "equanimity" towards Molly's infidelity and his arrival in the "promised land" of her warm, occupied bed. These events, the heart of Ithaca, are the soul of

Ulysses. Together they form the novel's central theme, examined later in detail: the theme of man's simultaneous isolation and community.

In addition to climactic importance, a second reason for selecting Ithaca for study is that the episode itself has often given rise to critical misunderstanding or even downright indignation. Joyce called it "the ugly duckling of the book."[2] Its question-and-answer technique, attitude of cold objectivity, freight of technical terms, labyrinthine sentence structure, ambiguity of theme and symbol—these and other matters have caused confusion. For many years, the chapter received scant critical attention, and only recently has any attempt been made at systematic examination of its textual evolution during the many stages of composition.

The following study is divided into two parts: textual and critical. The first part traces the growth of Ithaca from its infancy in Joyce's rough notes through the manuscript and typescript to full maturity in the final proofs. Here we explore materials and methods, trying to understand both artifact and artist better. The second part, on the other hand, shifting from textual reconstruction to critical consideration of the finished product, deals with such matters as Ithaca's meaning, structure, style, tone, rhythm, and language.

Each of these two parts illuminates the other. Critical understanding can throw light on the purpose of Joyce's textual alterations, and conversely, awareness of a textual change during composition can provide critical enlightenment in a given passage. As a result, the two parts cannot be kept completely separate; critical concerns will sometimes invade Part One, and textual references to notes or manuscripts will appear in Part Two. This synthesis of textual and critical approaches permits a fuller understanding not only of Ithaca, but of *Ulysses* and its author.

Part One

Evolution of the Text

1

The Background

The Sequence of Composition

The composition of Ithaca went through a series of nine or ten successive stages. Before dealing with any one of these, however, one must obtain an understanding of the entire process—its sequence, how one step derives from and leads to another, and exactly what materials are available for study. Scholars who concentrate on one stage without sufficient knowledge of the others are likely to draw incorrect or uncertain conclusions, or to encounter problems which are insoluble without an encompassing knowledge of the various textual versions. This was increasingly clear as Joyce's manuscripts became steadily more available for close study in such rich collections as those at the British Museum, Cornell, Yale, Harvard, the State University of New York at Buffalo, and the University of Texas.

The meaning of a passage in the final text may be confirmed, altered, or augmented when one finds, in an early manuscript, a rough note or germ idea, or sees that Joyce rejected, substituted, or added this or that phrase at precisely this or that point. For example, the final text records among Bloom's "infantile memories" of his daughter Milly that "she shook with shocks her moneybox: counted his three free moneypenny buttons one, tloo, tlee" (693; page references are to the 1961 reset Modern Library edition). On the surface this is merely an appealing onomatopoetic evocation of childhood with savings-bank and button game, but an entry in one of Joyce's notesheets, coupled with an addition to a galley proof, adds a new dimension. The rough note is "Milly mercenary—you want etwas," and the proof addition is the word "moneypenny," absent from earlier versions. Milly's monetary childhood occupations, in this light, reveal her as mercenary and demanding, a point Joyce underscored with the "moneypenny" addition. A different kind of enlightenment, this time confirmation of an uncertain allusion, can be found in the catalogue of the contents of Bloom's table drawer. We are twice told that part of an address from which Bloom has received pornographic articles is "Box 32" (721). The alert reader immediately recalls the 32 feet per second of Bloom's falling-body motif. Did Joyce definitely intend this correlation, or is the box number mere coincidence? The drafts reveal that nothing here is coincidental: in the basic manuscript the number is given as "Box 320" in both places; later in the proofs, Joyce carefully struck off the zero.

If this sort of before and after knowledge is helpful for full understanding of the final text, where all ends meet, it is sometimes mandatory for understanding any one separate draft prior to the published text, where ends are loose. The complicated matter of Joyce's system of using colored pencils in his notesheets, for instance, has intrigued all viewers. Incorrect guesses about it reveal that no answer is possible until several different stages of the text have been examined and compared. Study of just one or two drafts is not enough.

Actually, the Ithaca text passed through fewer stages than many other episodes did. For one thing, some episodes simply required more revision; Circe, which Joyce claimed to have rewritten some six or nine times (the figure varies), is an outstanding example. Again, Ithaca was not published separately in periodical form before appearance of the book, as were all other episodes up through part of Oxen of the Sun, and so of course lacks the typescript and proofsheets attending such publication. Finally, since Ithaca was the last episode to be finished and Joyce was working under severe pressure of time, he did not have as many proofs pulled as usual, contenting himself with two sets of galley proofs and one set of page proofs instead of the total of five or six for some other episodes.

Here, then, is the sequence of composition for Ithaca, which, with some modifications or additions, is also the sequence of most other episodes as well. Steps one and two, and possibly a third, involve preparation before actual composition begins. First Joyce jotted down ideas, catchwords, technical terms, scraps of conversation, phrases from advertisements, Dublin memories and the like, alert at all times for such potential material. He used envelopes, shirt cuffs, pocket pads, menus, small notebooks—anything available for receiving the rapid scrawl of his pencil, any place, any time. The best description of this process has been given by Joyce's painter friend, Frank Budgen, an eye- and ear-witness to much of it:

> Joyce was never without them...little writing blocks specially made for the waistcoat pocket. At intervals, alone or in conversation, seated or walking, one of these tablets was produced, and a word or two scribbled on it at lightning speed as ear or memory served his turn. No one knew how all this material was given place in the completed pattern of his work, but from time to time in Joyce's flat one caught glimpses of a few of

those big orange-coloured envelopes that are one of the glories of Switzerland, and these I always took to be storehouses of building material.

I have seen him collect in the space of a few hours the oddest assortment of material: a parody on the *House that Jack Built,* the name and action of a poison, the method of caning boys on training ships, the wobbly cessation of a tired, unfinished sentence, the nervous trick of a convive turning his glass in inward-turning circles, a Swiss musichall joke turning on a pun in Swiss dialect, a description of the Fitzsimmons shift.[3]

This method of accumulating material was by no means peculiar to the composition of *Ulysses.* Joyce used it from beginning to end of his career. His earliest "epiphanies" were little more than such observations carefully recorded. The notebook he kept in Paris during his first, interrupted flight from Dublin in 1903 contained long passages of such scraps and notations as Budgen describes.[4] Many of the published notes for *Exiles* are also of this nature, and some fifty small notebooks in the Lockwood Memorial Library at the University of Buffalo attest to Joyce's heavy reliance on this method in writing *Finnegans Wake.* As Harry Levin put it, "He has first to compile an exhaustive and matter-of-fact *dossier,* on the plane of objective description, that comes to the surface only in the Ithaca episode of [*Ulysses*]."[5]

As a second step Joyce classified these scattered notes according to the episodes for which they were intended, and transcribed them onto separate sheets or notebook pages headed with the names of those episodes. These pages he then kept beside him as he wrote, methodically crossing out each note with a colored pencil as he used it. Since not all cancelled notes found their way into the book, however, it is probable that another step, or intermediate semi-step, was involved: selection from these pages of certain notes he intended to use and their further transcription to another sheet. Thus a note crossed out when it was transferred as a probable building block to another sheet may still have been rejected later. It seems simplest, though, to consider this process of classified transcription as a single second step.

A third step, perhaps not taken with every episode but certainly with some, was the sketching of a rough outline of the main events or divisions of the episode — a crude road map for Joyce to steer his way through the first draft. This of course might well have been step one or two; it is placed third here simply because it seems to be most closely connected with the following first draft.

Step four, then, begins actual manuscript composition. Working usually in notebooks, Joyce wrote out his first draft, using the right-hand pages for the text proper and the left-hand for additions and revisions. For most episodes, he wrote only one rough draft and then moved ahead to the next step, but we cannot always be sure, where materials are lacking, that he did not write two or more drafts, as we know he did with Circe. It is therefore sometimes difficult or impossible to state certainly that this fourth step is a single link in the chain of composition; with multiple drafts, this stage could involve several steps.

Where there was only one rough draft, however, the next or fifth step was the fair copy for the typist. Here Joyce copied out his draft in clear, coherent form, making some revisions as he worked and expanding the text with additional material.

Steps six and seven concern the typescript. When the first copy came back from the typist, Joyce made still more revisions and additions. For pages where such alterations were few, there would be no second typescript; they were ready for the printer. Many pages, however, profusely covered with additions, required re-typing, and the resulting second typescript, or seventh step, went through the same process as the first typescript: some pages again were suitable for the printer, while others received a new burden of additions and went back to the typist. Thus for some pages there is a third typescript, but since Joyce, at least with Ithaca, made no changes in the third copy—time was running short—it does not constitute a separate step in composition.

The last three steps, so far as Ithaca is concerned, involve the printed proofs—as mentioned earlier, two galley proofs, and one page proof—on which Joyce again, as with the typescript, made more changes and additions. With more proofs, some other episodes went through five or six steps at this point.

A summary of Ithaca's sequence of composition, then, looks like this:

1. Slips with rough notes
2. Sheets of classified notes
(3. Outline of episode?)
4. Rough draft
5. Fair copy of rough draft
6. First typescript
7. Second typescript
8. First galley proof
9. Second galley proof
10. Page proof

Step three, the outline, has been questioned and placed in parentheses because such an outline for Ithaca has not turned up, and we cannot assume that Joyce used one here. It is certain, though, that Ithaca went through each of the other nine steps, even though the materials for two of them are missing. We do not have the original slips of rough notes (step 1) or the rough draft (step 4). The note slips, once they were classified and transcribed, were most probably destroyed; none of them appear to exist for any part of *Ulysses*. And where, as with Ithaca, we have the transcribed sheets, the loss is negligible. The missing rough draft, however, is a different matter.[6] It is obviously of great importance in the textual study of any episode, constituting as it does the earliest composed version. Where some intermediate draft is missing, such as a section of typescript, it is usually possible to reconstruct, by collation of preceding and following drafts, what happened in the missing portion.

This means that, except for the highly important notesheets, it is impossible to get behind the fair copy (Rosenbach manuscript) of Ithaca. We are denied the opportunity of watching Joyce at creative work *ab initio,* and if we can judge from extant drafts of other episodes, with their mass of cancellations, substitutions, and insertions, the Ithaca draft would yield rich results.

"Trieste-Zurich-Paris, 1914–1921": The Seventh Year

Joyce began serious work on Ithaca in February 1921; one year later, in February 1922, *Ulysses* was published. This was the seventh (and, actually, part of the eighth) year of work on the novel. What was Joyce's schedule of composition during this final period?

To trace the timetable of Ithaca we must turn back to the sixth year, when Joyce first referred to the final section of the book. In July 1920, at work on Circe, he wrote to Harriet Weaver, "A great part of the Nostos or close [i.e., Eumaeus, Ithaca and Penelope] was written several years ago and the style is quite plain."[7] This statement is puzzling. Joyce was probably referring here to rough notes, outlines, preliminary sketches and the like, rather than to any very definite composition, for certainly, with what we know of his laborious writing of the following year, no "great part" of the Nostos could have been composed earlier. And what Joyce means when he says "the style is quite plain" is anything but plain. Although he may possibly have meant "plain" to describe the cliché-ridden style of Eumaeus, the cold objectivity of Ithaca, and the fundamental frankness of Penelope, it sounds more like a statement made before he had worked out what are actually the highly involved styles in these episodes, especially the complexities of Ithaca. Probably the best interpretation is that, compared to the wild hallucinations of Circe, in which he was then embroiled, the style of the Nostos would be relatively unspectacular.

Whatever of the Nostos had actually been composed before 1921 most likely belonged to Eumaeus. In December 1920, with the Circe episode near completion, Joyce wrote Harriet Weaver, "The next one is already drafted,"8 and reminded Frank Budgen, in discussing the final episodes, work through one or more rough drafts, and arrived at a satisfactory to Budgen, after describing the style of Penelope, Joyce said, "...there remains only to think out Ithaca in the way I suggest." His wording here implies previous ideas and conversations, but it is clear that at the end of 1920 much of Ithaca's plan was yet to be formulated.

The basic draft of Circe was completed before Christmas of 1920. Joyce immediately turned his full attention to Eumaeus and, working rapidly, finished it about mid-February, 1921. Without pause he proceeded to Ithaca. From then until August we hear occasional references to the episode (by April, for example, he had written "a good part of *Ithaca*"10 and in early June he could tell Valery Larbaud that "*Ithaca* is progressing rapidly"11 yet moan later in the same month to Frank Budgen that "*Ithaca* is giving me fearful trouble"12), but nothing specific. He was now working on Penelope at the same time, and by early August we get fairly definite news on both episodes: "I have the greater part of *Ithaca* but it has got to be completed, revised and rearranged above all on account of its scheme. I have also written the first sentence of Penelope but as this contains about 2,500 words the deed is more than it seems to be."13 We cannot be sure just what "the greater part" mentioned here consisted of, but it seems likely that in the six months since February, together with work on Penelope and non-literary activities, Joyce had arranged and transcribed his Ithaca notes, worked through one or more rough drafts, and arrived at a satisfactory basic version of the episode. The completion, revision and rearrangement he mentions as still lying ahead probably involved making the fair copy, with its extensive additions, which later became the Rosenbach manuscript.

During August and September Joyce abandoned Ithaca, working instead full time on Penelope. After six months of Ithaca, and with that episode in fairly advanced shape, Joyce undoubtedly welcomed the complete change in mood and method offered by Molly Bloom's soliloquy. But there was also a more compelling reason for the switch. On December 7, Valery Larbaud was to lecture on *Ulysses* at Adrienne Monnier's bookshop, and parts of the novel, including Penelope, were to be read aloud. Penelope thereby took priority, to allow time for its French translation and to let Larbaud know how the book ended. By the first week in October Joyce had completed not only the fair copy of Penelope but had revised the typescript as well, for the episode was then at the printer's.

October was spent in completing the fair copy of Ithaca. Although he told Miss Weaver on October 7 that "I am very slow and have just enough energy to write the dry rocks pages of *Ithaca*,"14 he could turn around and tell Robert McAlmon three days later, "Have sent the first part of *Ithaca* to the typist and am working like a lunatic trying to revise and improve and connect and continue and create all at the one time." [15] Certainly the enervated lament here to Miss Weaver, if true at all, was only a very temporary mood; Joyce was furiously—and happily—bringing his Irish stew to a boil. At any rate, on October 29 he announced to McAlmon, "I have just finished the *Ithaca* episode so that at last the writing of *Ulysses* is finished. I have still a lot of proofreading and revising to do but the composition is at an end." [16] Joyce had written, revised, and sent to the typist his last fair copy of the novel.

Composition may have been "at an end" for most of the book, but certainly not for Ithaca. Thirty-four percent of that episode was composed in additions to its typescript and proofs. Indeed, Joyce continued even at this late date to collect information he could use. On November 2 he wrote the famous note to his Aunt Josephine Murray asking whether an ordinary person could perform Bloom's feat of dropping into the front area of 7 Eccles Street, explaining that "I require this information in detail in order to determine the wording of a paragraph." [17] He evidently received and used this information, for the paragraph in the manuscript makes no mention of a "dwarf wall" and "stiles" (668), inserted later in the typescript. He also wrote Frank Budgen at this time, requesting catalogues on home furnishings, old books and stamp collecting, all used in Ithaca.

During November, then, Joyce labored over the revision of the typescript. No evidence reveals just when it went to the printer, but early December is a good guess, for the first Ithaca galley proof bears the rubber stamp, "IMPRIMERIE DARANTIERE DIJON," with the date "15 Décembre 1921."

Correcting and revising proofs of *Ulysses* was by now, of course, a wearily familiar task: along with the composition of Ithaca and Penelope, Joyce had been working with galley proofs since the previous June and with page proofs since September. Now, in December, just several days before receiving the first Ithaca proofs, he complained to Miss Weaver, "...the printer, for some reason, sends me now proofs of *Circe, Eumaeus* and *Penelope* at the same time without having finished the composition of the first two and I have to work on them simultaneously, different as they are." [18] Joyce thus spent the last days of 1921 besieged by the page proofs for several different episodes as well as by the Ithaca galleys.

The achievement of the Darantiere Press in publishing *Ulysses* on Joyce's fortieth birthday, February 2, 1922, is a little short of miraculous when one realizes that the author was still revising proofs—not merely correcting but, as always, adding new material—almost to the end of the preceding month. The last page proofs were pulled on January 19 and 20 (dated on proofs by printer's stamp); when these were returned corrected, they were dated again, and the last of the Ithaca proofs were received by the printer on January 27. Indeed, the last page proof for the book — the concluding pages of Penelope — is dated by the printer January 31, 1922 — two days before publication! (Compare his letter of the same day to Frank Budgen: "I have been working on the last proofs till this morning." [19]) Even after the last Ithaca proofs had left Joyce's hands, probably about January 25, he *still* revised them. In red ink on the last proof a printer has substituted the word "(atonement)" for "(peace offering)" (729), and noted in the margin, "lettre de M. Joyce reçue 30.1.22." Rarely in publishing history can the phrase "last-minute changes" have so closely approached literal truth.

The seventh year, therefore, saw the revision of the Circe typescript, the composition of the last three episodes and revision of their typescripts, and the revision of the entire book in galley and page proofs — a busy enough twelve or thirteen months. But much else was also happening. There were preparations for the Larbaud lecture, especially collaboration in translating sections to be read. There were two changes in living quarters, as Joyce first moved into Larbaud's flat in June, and then, when the poet-critic returned from Italy in October, back to the previous residence at 9 rue de l'Université. There were difficulties in finding shock-proof typists for the Fescennine Circe, in rewriting a section of that episode which was destroyed, in trying to find a publisher for *Ulysses*. There was the trial, which Joyce followed closely, of the *Little Review* for printing the Nausicaa episode. And there was his health. He fainted once in July and again in August. In early July he suffered a severe eye attack and work halted entirely for five weeks of recuperation. All in all, one marvels that the end of *Ulysses* was not also the end of its author.

2

The Rough Notes

For some years, Joyce's rough notes for *Ulysses* remained largely unexplored territory, receiving very little critical attention. Now they have been published in both annotated transcription[1] and facsimile,[2] and all serious critics are aware of their importance.

Perhaps some of the early neglect of these notes may be blamed on the difficulty of reading them. Joyce's handwriting and his practice of heavily crossing out notes with colored pencils are indeed barriers, but they are not so insuperable as they may at first seem. Although many of the notes are wholly or partially illegible — indeed, sometimes actually invisible under the colored penciling — by far the great majority of them can be deciphered, but no one who has worked with them can deny that they demand almost prohibitive quantities of time and patience.

Depending on the circumstances, Joyce actually wrote three different handwriting styles, which might be labelled his "personal," "publication," and "epistolary" hands. The "personal" hand Joyce used when writing for his own eyes only. It is the handwriting of the notes and rough drafts, and even with considerable practice any reader will have hard going with it. And why not, when it occasionally gave Joyce himself trouble? Frank Budgen recalls the time Joyce asked him to decipher some scribbles on a note slip, saying, "I can't make head or tail of it." But even after using a magnifying glass Budgen was forced to reply, "I can't make out one complete word."[3] Sylvia Beach has remarked, "Joyce's handwriting, which had once been quite legible, was getting, with its ellipses and barely perceptible signs, to be as difficult to read as ogham."[4]

Miss Beach was mistaken, however, in assuming that Joyce's handwriting had decayed to this point from an earlier legibility. He could still be beautifully legible when he wanted to, and he very much wanted to whenever he was transcribing his text for either typists' or printers' eyes — his "publication" hand. A schoolchild would have no difficulty with the handwriting in Joyce's fair copies and on his typescripts and proofsheets. Every letter is perfectly formed. This clear, almost classic, hand wherever publication was involved is precisely what might be expected from the artist who took utmost pains to insure that his works be exactly as he wanted them. Anyone who owns a copy of *Ulysses* has a specimen of this hand: the words accompanying the music of the Hugh of Lincoln ballad in Ithaca (690–91) were written by Joyce himself, although their reproduction is not of the best.[5]

The "epistolary" hand is the handwriting of Joyce's letters, or of instructions to printers on his proofsheets. It falls midway between the "personal" and "publication" hands, far more legible than the former but lacking the careful clarity of the latter.

Working with Joyce's rough notes, then, means groping one's way laboriously from entry to entry, confronting literally hundreds of calligraphic problems on almost every page. Many hours are required to transcribe one page of these notes, and even then blank spaces must be left or uncertain words stigmatized with question marks. When one realizes that for Ithaca alone there exist some twenty pages of notes, it is not difficult to understand why their detailed examination was delayed.

Joyce made two different collections of Ithaca notes. By far the more important of these are sixteen pages, contained in six separate sheets, which were given to the British Museum by Harriet Weaver. These are part of a series of notesheets sent to Miss Weaver by Paul Léon in 1938, evidently at Joyce's request. In all there are twenty-nine separate sheets, dealing with the last seven episodes of *Ulysses*.[6] Eighteen of the sheets have been folded once to produce four pages each, while the other eleven are single, or two pages each—a total of some ninety sides or pages of notes, with a few blank pages. The sheets are distributed among the episodes as follows: Cyclops—3, Nausicaa—2, Oxen of the Sun—6, Circe—7, Eumaeus—3, Ithaca—6, Penelope—2.

Two of the six Ithaca sheets are double, or four pages each; the other four sheets are single, written on both sides. Joyce entered his notes on these sixteen pages in roughly columnar form, sometimes making two neat columns per page, but more often starting off with a single column and then adding notes wherever space permitted on the right side of the page or in the left margin. The number of separate entries per page ranges from sixty-five to about two hundred, and the entries themselves range from single words or mathematical symbols to small paragraphs of several elliptical sentences. All told, these British Museum notesheets for Ithaca contain about 1,700 entries, and of these about two-thirds have been crossed out with colored pencil.

Joyce was both meticulous and thorough in his cancellation of notes. He did not slash through them carelessly, but, to the exasperation of the scholar, placed colored lines with almost engineering precision through the center of his entries. Although he did not always use every note he crossed out, he almost never, on the other hand, used a note without cancelling it. Very rarely, it seems, he slipped. The term "fire brasses," for example, appears uncancelled among other notes for Bloom's dreamhouse, yet "massive firebrasses" are among the furnishings in the text (713). Or again, there is the uncancelled phrase, "Wren's auction, little statue," yet standing on Bloom's table is "an image of Narcissus purchased by auction from P. A. Wren, 9 Bachelor's Walk" (710). Sometimes he would cancel only part of a note, rejecting the rest: in the entry "A smile goes a long way with a woman," the first six words are crossed out but not the last three, and sure enough, in the Hades episode appears only "A smile goes a long way" (93).

Dating the notesheets is difficult. About the best that can be done is to place them fairly certainly within a period from 1919 to 1921.[7] A. Walton Litz arrived at 1919 as the earlier date by noting that entries from the sheets applying to earlier episodes were not used in the versions of those episodes published in the *Little Review* or *The Egoist* in 1918 and early 1919. The notes, therefore, were most probably compiled and used after serial publication, or during the last two or two-and-a-half years of composition.

Some notes are very broad or general, probably early entries made before Joyce had worked out fuller details, suggesting that the Ithaca notes were compiled over a course of months or even years. Such an entry, for example, as "Mrs. Riordan in bath chair," the basis for a whole question in the final text, is clearly only a reminder or "key," requiring later amplification. Other entries, however, are very exact or particular, such as "Put Molly in dairy—what to do with our wives." Here Joyce was obviously accumulating material for a question conceived earlier. Sometimes the notes contain both a general entry for a question and specific details for the same question. Thus the note "LB's favourite dream" is probably an early entry, while such notes as "bathroom (h & c) 999 years," "tiled kitchen," "cozy corner fitment" and many others represent a later collection of furnishings for Saint Leopold's dream cottage.

Joyce used these notes for every stage or version of Ithaca, raiding them no fewer than seven different times and perhaps more, depending on whether more than one draft was written before the Rosenbach manuscript. In addition, he also resorted to them at other times, for some sixty entries from the Ithaca sheets were used in other episodes. Here is a tabulation of the cancelled Ithaca notes that have been traced to the final text, showing the various drafts to which they were added:

Basic manuscript	396
Additions to manuscript	57

First typescript	110
Second typescript	56
First galley proof	20
Second galley proof	31
Page proof	12
Other episodes of book	60

Of the several hundred remaining cancelled entries, many were not used in the book and some are indecipherable. There are also some duplicate entries, and some that appear several times in the final text, so that it is impossible to assign them to any one draft.

Joyce had these notes by him when he was making final additions to the text only days before publication. The question in which Bloom, talking to Stephen, decides to suppress a "statement explanatory of his absence on the occasion of the interment of Mrs. Mary Dedalus" (695) was added to a final page proof dated by the printer as having been returned to him on January 27, 1922. And this question had its source in the notesheet entry, "LB *not* at funeral of SD's mother."

The other repository of Ithaca notes is a small forty-page notebook (some pages are blank) at Buffalo. Lacking covers, and in extremely fragile condition, the book contains notes for some ten episodes, entered not in columnar form but consecutively across the page and separated by commas.[8] There are three full pages of Ithaca notes, plus a fourth page with only eight entries—a total of 342 notes, of which 199 have been crossed out in color.

The date of this notebook falls within the same 1919–21 period as the British Museum notesheets, but with strong evidence that it was compiled later than most of the notesheets. For one thing, it is almost completely lacking in the kind of general or "germ" notes that abound in the notesheets. That is, instead of notes on which whole questions or even series of questions were founded, the notebook contains only very precise terms, usually single words or short phrases. Here Joyce gathered small supporting details for the larger framework, already mapped out. For example, of the notes actually used in the text, nearly sixty, or more than a third, supplied additions to four consecutive questions about Bloom's dreamhouse (beginning with "In what ultimate ambition had all concurrent and consecutive ambitions now coalesced?" 712). Obviously the collection of what Wyndham Lewis called "an Aladdin's cave of incredible bric-a-brac...into which several encyclopaedias have been emptied"[9] was a major purpose of these notes, intended to supplement the even larger collection of the notesheets.

A guess about those "encyclopaedias" may suggest a date very late indeed for some of these notes. On November 6, 1921, Joyce wrote to

Frank Budgen asking if he would like to see some extracts from Ithaca, adding, "I have still some weeks' work of revision and proofreading to do." He then asked Budgen to send him, "as quickly as possible registered," several handbooks and manuals, including "Any catalogue of Whiteley's or Harrod's stores," and "Any catalogue of Tottenham Court Road furnishers."[10] Many of the dreamhouse furnishings in these notes were most probably copied at this time from these catalogues, especially since many were crammed into the pages in the margins or at the bottoms at last-minute additions.

Strengthening these considerations is the fact that this Buffalo notebook, unlike the notesheets, was not used during the composition of Ithaca's rough draft or fair copy. It was first used in the first typescript, on which Joyce was working when he wrote the above letter to Budgen. He returned to the notebook for the second typescript and first galley proof, and then discarded it except for a couple of entries in the final page proof. Distribution of the notebook entries among the drafts is as follows:

First typescript	50
Second typescript	32
First galley proof	60
Second galley proof	0
Page proof	2
Other episodes of book	3

With this evidence that the notebook was probably compiled and certainly used later than the British Museum notesheets, it can be dated more exactly. As seen earlier, Joyce began serious work on Ithaca in February 1921, and the manuscript was finished and at the typist's by the end of October of that year. During this period of composing rough draft and fair copy, Joyce used the notesheets heavily, but made no use of the notebook; it emerges only during the typescript and proof work of November and December. If his thorough use of the notesheets is any criterion, he would surely have made similar use of the notebook if it existed. Most probably, then, it was compiled only after Joyce was well into Ithaca, and was intended as a reservoir of additional details for later stages of composition. All the evidence points to the summer and fall of 1921.[11]

In addition to the British Museum notesheets and Buffalo notebook, Joyce actually made a third collection of Ithaca notes—after *Ulysses* was published. At Buffalo is a very large bound notebook, ledger-like in outward appearance but with unlined pages numbered in pencil right up to the last page facing the back cover—1,018 pages in all. The book has obviously seen heavy duty: the spinal binding is missing and the durable covers are considerably scuffed. Scattered throughout its pages at widely separated intervals are notes under headings for every one of Joyce's works up through *Ulysses: Chamber Music,* the stories of *Dubliners, A Portrait, Exiles,* and each episode of *Ulysses.* At the beginning is also a section of personal, diary-like notes, such as "Drunk again for a change."

Page 851 of this notebook is headed "Ithaca," filled with 127 notes in Joyce's cryptic "personal" hand. Only twenty-nine of these are crossed out in color. The immediately following several pages contain a transcription of the notes in the large, clear handwriting of Mme France Raphael, "whose duty," Richard Ellmann tells us, "it was to copy in large letters his almost illegible notations."[12] Joyce had crossed out the twenty-nine entries before she transcribed the notes, for she omits them.

A mere glance at the color scheme gives warning that something here is "wrong." Whereas entries in the notesheets and small notebook are can- celled only in blue, red or green, these are cancelled in orange, brown or green. And a study of the contents soon reveals that not a single entry, crossed or uncrossed, can be traced to Ithaca—or to any other episode. These notes, clearly, played no part in the composition of *Ulysses.* And with good reason. In the years immediately following publication of that novel, Joyce was here beginning to recruit troops for the battle of *Finne- gans Wake.* All this was made clear when Thomas Connolly edited and transcribed this book in *Scribbledehobble: The Ur-Workbook for "Finne- gans Wake."*[13] ("Scribbledehobble" is Joyce's first entry in the notebook.)

Even though these Ithaca notes were never intended for nor used in that episode, they are worth some attention here. A. Walton Litz, noting the headings for each of Joyce's works up to and including the chapters of *Ulysses,* writes that "the obvious aim was to make one level of *Finnegans Wake* a summing-up of his artistic career,"[14] and Connolly points out the thematic or stylistic similarity of each section of notes to the title in the heading. In short, the Ithaca notes here provide us with Joyce's *post facto* view of the episode he had written. If he were to evoke the ghost of Ithaca, what should he stress? Science and technology, of course, are very much present, but these entries might better be described as featuring big words and odd facts. Here are such Ithacan beauties as *uranographical, pantech- nicon, anaglyptographic, paraphes, nephoscope, armamentarium, rhinen- cephalon,* and others. As for odd facts, Joyce has carefully recorded such things as "man blindfold returns to self in field because right step is bigger," "man on tightrope a 1 dim. being," "telegraph wires embrace earth," and "iron ore deflects wireless."

Sixteen pages on loose sheets and a little over three pages in a small notebook are the rough notes Joyce collected for Ithaca's questions and answers. All together, used and unused, they comprise a staggering total of more than 2,000 separate entries. (Enough, had they all been used, to have supplied Ithaca with more than twenty-five notes per page.) Before examining the nature and use of the notes in more detail, however, one must consider a matter as tantalizing as it is important. This is Joyce's system of crossing out notes in color as he used them.

Early in October 1921, while working on the manuscript of Ithaca, Joyce wrote to Harriet Weaver: "A few lines to let you know I am here again with MSS and pencils (red, green and blue)..." [15] Although he used other colors in other episodes, the Ithaca notes display only red, green, and blue. Such a literally colorful method of operation naturally attracted attention, but surmises about it suffered from lack of detailed information. Valery Larbaud commented that Joyce's text "is a genuine example of the art of mosaic. I have seen the drafts. They are entirely composed of abbreviated phrases underlined in various-coloured pencils. These are annotations intended to recall to the author complete phrases; and the pencil-marks indicate according to their colour that the underlined phrase belongs to such or such an episode. It makes one think of the boxes of little coloured cubes of the mosaic workers." [16] Sylvia Beach agreed with him on the function of the colors: "He used...pencils of different colors to distinguish the parts he was working on." [17]

This "episodic" explanation of the colors may to some extent have been true for some episodes, but it does not hold for Ithaca at all. The difficulty is obvious: Ithacan entries were crossed out in red, green, or blue; how then could these same colors distinguish entries used in other episodes? A brief statistical check makes it clear that Joyce did not use color according to episodes. Ten entries from the notesheets, for example, found their way into Penelope, written simultaneously with Ithaca. Eight of these were crossed out in blue, the other two in red, but since blue and red were used for hundreds of notes in Ithaca itself, the Penelope entries gain no distinction, blending chameleon-like into the surrounding Ithacan landscape. The same is true of notes used in other episodes. In fact, the three colors were used for non-Ithaca notes in roughly the same proportion as for Ithaca itself:

	Notes used in other episodes	Notes used in Ithaca
Blue:	70%	61%
Red:	23%	35%
Green:	7%	4%

Only a thorough knowledge of *Ulysses* and the aid of Hanley's *Word Index,* not dependence on color, will serve in identifying the emigrants among the Ithaca notes. [18]

Since the varied colors do not differentiate Ithaca from other episodes, their function must lie solely within the limits of Ithaca itself. In tracing notes as they appear in the successive stages of manuscript, type-script and proofs, one soon becomes aware that certain colors dominate certain drafts. For example, an unmistakable majority of notes used in the basic manuscript were crossed out in blue, whereas red was the cancelling color for most of the notes used in the typescript. This system does not hold absolutely true—there are significant and puzzling exceptions. But some definite patterns are clearly discernible.

Here is a color portrait of the different drafts:

	Notes cancelled in:		
	Blue	**Red**	**Green**
Basic manuscript	87%	12%	1%
Additions to manuscript	48%	50%	2%
First and second typescript	10%	85%	5%
First galley proof	66%	5%	29%
Second galley proof	36%	61%	3%
Page proof	35%	18%	47%

In working through the versions, therefore, Joyce shifted colors in this pattern:

Blue

Blue-Red

Red

Blue-Green

Red-Blue

Green-Blue-Red

But if these statistics show that Joyce, to one extent or another, varied his colors according to his drafts, they also raise some obvious questions. Why, in some versions, are two colors used prominently, such as the blue and red of the manuscript additions, or the blue and green of the first galley proof? And why, in other versions where one color is dominant, are there nevertheless significant minorities of other colors, such as the 12 percent red in the otherwise blue manuscript, or the 10 percent blue in the dominantly red typescript?

A fairly definite answer is possible in at least one case. A galley proof for the whole of Ithaca consisted of eight large sheets, or "placards" as the French printers called them, and in the first galley proof Joyce seems to have varied his colors according to the different placards. At this stage the dominant colors are blue (66 percent) and green (29 percent), and when the notes are traced to the placards a color pattern unmistakably emerges, despite some inconsistencies:

Placard	Notes
1	11 green, 1 red
2	5 blue, 1 red
3	7 green
4	9 blue, 2 red
5	7 blue, 1 red
6	22 blue
7	3 blue, 1 red, 1 green
8	2 blue

Except for the last two placards, where the numbers are inconclusive, this summary reveals that although blue governs most of the placards, the notes for the first and third were cancelled in green. There is no apparent reason for this: the "green" notes are not closely related in content, they are drawn from widely separated places in the notesheets and small Buffalo notebook, and they are added to many different questions within the two placards. Moreover, whatever his purpose was in shifting color according to placard in this first galley proof, Joyce did not do this in the second galley proof or page proof, where colors are mixed so arbitrarily that no pattern is apparent.

The theory, then, that different colors indicate different stages of composition and, in the first galley proof, different placards, creates as many problems as it solves. That some such pattern is present the evidence clearly shows, but the inconsistencies cannot be ignored, and the problem is only partly solved.

So far, the assumption has been that Joyce crossed over his notes as he transferred them directly from notesheets or notebook to his text. But suppose, instead, that before using his notes he first copied them on to other sheets. There is no concrete evidence that he did this, but the circumstantial evidence is tempting, and the theory goes far to explain those mystifying inconsistencies. Suppose that before beginning composition Joyce went carefully through his notes twice. The first time he collected on separate sheets all those notes he needed for the first draft, arranging or grouping them roughly in desired order. As he copied them down, he crossed out the original notes in blue. The second time through he copied, on different sheets, those notes to be used later for expanding the draft, this time cancelling the originals in red. These "secondary" notes could be conveniently omitted from the basic draft, to be fitted into its established framework during revision. Here, for example, would be many of the various water, mathematical and astronomical terms. Now Joyce has two collections of notes, one of basic or structural materials, the other of important, but not immediately necessary addenda. He puts aside the original notesheets and the deferred "red" list, concentrates on the basic "blue" list, and begins to write. Occasionally, however, he finds immediate use for something in the red list; more rarely, he even turns back to the original notesheets for a suddenly desirable note, and when he does this he crosses out the original in green. And so he works not only through the first draft, but through all succeeding versions, plundering the blue and red lists as he wishes. The first version is of course predominantly "blue" (basic manuscript 87 percent blue). For the additions to the manuscript he continues to use the blue list, but also decides to add here a number of water terms, especially to the "water hymn" near the beginning (manuscript additions 48 percent blue, 50 percent red — and of the twenty-eight notes from the red list, no less than twenty-five concern water).

At this point, with the manuscript behind him, Joyce is ready to add to his two working lists the notes from the small notebook, compiled expressly for the typescript and proof work which now lies immediately ahead. Most of these notes, as one might expect from their detailed nature, are added to the secondary red list, and it is this list he next concentrates on for the typescript (85 percent red). In the first galley proof he not only returns mainly to the blue list (66 percent blue, 5 percent red), but now also makes a determined third search of the original notesheets (29 percent green). The second galley and final page proofs receive an assortment culled from all three sources.

Hypothetical as this reconstruction necessarily is, it has much to commend it. With it, we are spared the improbable picture of Joyce, while composing, juggling three colored pencils besides his regular writing pencil, and searching repeatedly through many pages of more or less disorganized notes to assemble those he needs. Instead, he has already organized the notes in copying them, and of course can cross out the transcribed entries in any way he likes, most probably with his writing pencil. The theory also explains why we find multiple colors among notes used in the same draft: Joyce did not cancel here in blue and there in red and here again in green, all without any evident purpose; he simply selected from transcribed lists made one at a time, one color at a time. Finally, it explains the fate of the many cancelled notes *not* used in the text. If Joyce cancelled each note as he used it directly in composition, why are these notes missing from the novel? But if he cancelled them while making a second list, intending to use them but later deciding not to, then of course all is clear.

This conjecture that Joyce worked with transcribed lists instead of with the original notes thus not only answers the puzzling questions raised by the color scheme, but turns a subject which at first seemed only to obscure matters into a means of gaining increased understanding about Joyce's habits of composition. Most important, perhaps, is the evidence that Joyce deliberately paced himself by ignoring much available material in composing his basic version, saving it instead for later stages where he could turn his attention to the tasks of expansion, illustration and sharpening of detail. Indeed, considering the fact that Ithaca contains far more concrete details than any other episode, one can easily understand why Joyce made no attempt to cope with all his material when he set to work. With characteristic methodical practicality, he divided and conquered, exercising full control over his art at every point.

The notes themselves fall into several distinct categories. The most important entries created whole questions in the final text. The central idea or action of some eighty-five questions can be traced, in each instance, to a single note. A few entries of this sort were already fairly well developed, and required relatively little alteration or expansion in order to take their place in the text. On the left below, for example, is Bloom's "missing-person" advertisement in note form, with the final version on the right:

£5 reward, missing gent aged about 40 height 5, 8, full build, dark complexion. May have since grown a beard. Was dressed when last seen. Above will be paid for his discovery.	£5 reward lost, stolen or strayed from his residence 7 Eccles street, missing gent about 40, answering to the name of Bloom, Leopold (Poldy), height 5 ft. 9 1-2 inches, full build, olive complexion, may have since grown a beard, when last seen was wearing a black suit. Above sum will be paid for information leading to his discovery. (727)

Litz has pointed out that in the note Joyce omitted such easily supplied details as name and address, and in the final version altered the text to resemble a "missing-animal" advertisement, with its "lost, stolen or strayed" and "answering to the name of."[19] Joyce himself may have lost something, however, when he conventionalized the note's "Was dressed when last seen."

Some of the form for the missing-person ad probably was copied from an actual source, for in other cases where Joyce quotes ads or documents he has taken careful notes. The longest of all the notes, for instance, concerns the Wonderworker prospectus in Bloom's table drawer. Here Joyce recorded an entry of 123 words, obviously copied from an actual advertisement, detailing the marvels of the "world's greatest remedy for rectal complaints," including the testimonial about the South African campaign. The note, almost unchanged, forms two questions and part of a third in the final text (722). Again, Joyce was careful to obtain the correct legal phrasing for Rudolph Virag's change-of-name notice (723), setting down the following note.

> Notice of change of name
> I, R. V. now; resid, formerly of: hereby give notice that I have assumed & intend henceforth upon all occasions & at all times

Most of the notes producing whole questions, however, are simply short, elliptical statements rarely exceeding half a dozen words. Many are merely plot indicators, so to speak, glossing basic actions in the episode:

> LB locked out
> LB washes under tap
> SD recites verse
> LB & SD see shooting star
> LB in dark bumps side
> LB tells of wonderful friend

Such entries, here arranged in chronological order, are scattered without order through the notes, apparently written down as they occurred to Joyce. Occasionally an entry reveals that he had in mind a series of questions, such as "SD's story. 'Queen's Hotel' LB coincidence" producing the four-question sequence in which Stephen's epiphany of the solitary girl writing in the Queen's Hotel reminds Bloom of his father's suicide there; startled, Bloom dismisses the connection as a coincidence (684–85).

Many entries contain just enough to remind Joyce of his intention. "Sinbad sailer [sic], Jinbad jailer etc" reveals that Joyce had already worked out Bloom's go-to-sleep reverie (737), and needed only a reminder. The questions detailing Bloom's athletic endeavors grow from the note, "indoor exercise" (681). "Mack Intosh," "Belles of George's," "cold of space," "pyramid of incense," "disasters influence"—each generates a separate question. "Did you tell me or I you?" is all Joyce needed for a description of one of Bloom's confused moments:

> Why did Bloom refrain from stating that he had frequented the university of life?

> Because of his fluctuating incertitude as to whether this observation had or had not been already made by him to Stephen or by Stephen to him. (682)

The succinct "Space reversible time no" results in the following:

What would render such return irrational?

An unsatisfactory equation between an exodus and return in time through reversible space and an exodus and return in space through irreversible time. (728)

Pleased at his favorable reception by several women during the day, Bloom is led to dream about "The possibility of exercising virile power of fascination in the most immediate future after an expensive repast in a private apartment in the company of an elegant courtesan, of corporal beauty, moderately mercenary, variously instructed, a lady by origin." (722) The source for this erotic extravaganza? No more than "LB & flash whore."

In compiling these notes, Joyce was not always sure which episode would be the beneficiary of this or that particular deposit. For example, as noted above, "Did you tell me or I you?" reached its amplified avatar in Ithaca, but it had to wait for the chance: in the Cyclops notesheets is "Did I say to him or he to me?" and the Eumaeus notes include "Did you say to me or I to you?" Or again, Molly's arrangement of the furniture, a prominent feature of Ithaca, was earlier considered for mention (but not mentioned) in both Nausicaa ("Change of furniture. LB foresees." and on another sheet "Molly will change furniture") and Circe ("Molly will change furniture."). Like his own uncertain or dissatisfied characters, Joyce questioned and experimented.

Many other notes, not pregnant enough to become entire questions, nevertheless form important parts of questions:

> They saw same cloud
> he knew that he knew that he knew
> RB bought straw hat
> MB wrote Greek
> Milly rattling moneybox
> LB finds 1/- in waistcoat
> RB drank soup from plate

Many of Bloom's get-rich-quick schemes are found in such notes:

> LB broke bank
> LB found ring in fowl
> LB with dogvan
> enclose the Bull
> Harness Poulapouca
> Blum Pascha dies & leaves LB big fortune

Comparison between the irreducible minimum of the notes and the unsurpassable maximum of the text emphasizes how Joyce has inflated his simple entries into the ludicrously pretentious jargon of Ithaca. The notes on the left below become, in the text, the monstrosities on the right:

girl's backside open LB follows bum	the posterior interstice of the imperfectly occluded skirt of a carnose negligent perambulating female (727)
LB shaves eves day you don't shave meet girl	[Shaving at night produced] a softer skin if unexpectedly encountering female acquaintances in remote places at incustomary hours (674)
Man lifted out of earth atmosph. bleeds at nose	the human organism... when elevated to a considerable altitude in the terrestrial atmosphere suffered... from nasal hemorrhage (699–700)

Joyce sometimes shamelessly exaggerated his material. Somewhere, for example, he had picked up and recorded the astronomical oddity, "See star by day from bottom of gully." But for Bloom, pointing out the constellations to Stephen, this is far too unimpressive; accordingly, he speaks of the milky way as "discernible by daylight by an observer placed at the lower end of a cylindrical vertical shaft 5000 ft deep sunk from the surface towards the centre of the earth" (698).

Still another kind of note is the concrete noun, sometimes accompanied by an adjective or two: *cataract, Saturn's ring, sectional bookcase, Old bazaar ticket, Maria Theresia.* These names of persons, places, and things were usually collected for a definite place in the text, such as one of the four long catalogues on water (671–72), the constellations (700–701), the dreamhouse (712–13), and Bloom's locked table drawer (720–21). Indeed, a total of more than 170 separate notes went into these four questions alone (the sixty-two notes used in the "water hymn" represent an average of one note for approximately every eight words). Some entries, however, such as *fulcrum, crater, barrel of key, ordnance map,* were collected with no definite position in mind, and were inserted in the text wherever Joyce believed them suitable.

Finally, there are the hundreds of abstract nouns, prepositional or conjunctive phrases, verbs, adjectives, adverbs, etc., almost all captured helter-skelter in Joyce's net to be released throughout Ithaca in positive swarms. One is surprised, though, after fighting through the episode's sesquipedalian vocabulary and overcoming such linguistic terrors as *boustrophedontic, luteofulvous, diathermanous, rhabdomantic, quinquecostate,* and many others, to discover an almost total absence of big words in the notes.[20] Certainly, it would seem, Joyce would be on the lookout for these. Yet except for *homothetic, thaumaturgic, ipsorelative* and *aliorelative,* the vocabulary of the notes would cause the average college sophomore little trouble. Joyce simply did not need to record such jawbreakers: the master linguist could produce any number of them whenever he liked. What he was more interested in, however, and what was for him not so easy, was to lard Ithaca with the workaday, journeyman jargon of the sciences, particularly mathematics, logic, astronomy, and physics. As a result, the notes are glutted with really elementary technical terms. One finds scores of such phrases as the following:

> state of rest
> thing in itself
> Satisfy equation
> no last term
> exert force
> cent per cent
> describe a circle
> greater lesser in equality
> raise to n^{th} power
> which is absurd

Joyce was not sure of himself here, and required the support of extensive notation. This does not mean, of course, that he did not know these and far more specialized terms, but it does mean that Joyce, who after all was composing a parody of scientific language, was not in his natural element. The artist had to become pseudo-scientist, and his uneasiness is clearly revealed as he speaks about Ithaca in a letter to Harriet Weaver: "The episode should be read by some person who is a physicist, mathematician and astronomer and a number of other things. I hope to find one however."[21] His great mass of notes on what is actually little more than high school science is what we might expect of the parodist who studied cheap romantic fiction for the language of Gerty MacDowell and plundered pornography for the perversions of Circe. The Ithaca notes, in short, are vivid proof that Joyce steeped himself in scientific terminology, raiding basic textbooks and manuals for the idioms of geometry ("sides about the angles"), algebra ("$abc = bac = cab$"), trigonometry ("4 is log of 81 to base 3"), mechanics ("arms of lever"), thermodynamics ("thermal unit raise 1 lb of H_2O 1 F"), astronomy ("light from polestar 36 years"), and many other subjects. Even characters are regarded mathematically: "LB tangent" or (whatever this means) "SD radius vector LB & SD = 0." Not even the Redeemer is exempt: "$JC = 3\sqrt{God}$." Entry after entry records mathematical formulae or equations, most of which, Joyce must have known, could not possibly be used in the final text, and many of which seem little more than numerical doodling. In the margin of some page we find this consecutive series:

$$a + b - c = b + a - c$$
$$a + b - c = b + a - c$$
$$abb + (-c) = b - (+c) + a$$
$$ax^3 = 4 \text{ dimensions}$$
$$a^6 \times a^4b^2 + b^6$$

On another page Joyce plays with progressions:

1	2	3	4	5	6	7	8	9

$$1 = \tfrac{1}{2} \times \tfrac{1}{4} \times \tfrac{1}{8} \times \tfrac{1}{16} \sim \infty$$

0	1	2	3	4	5	6	7	8	9
1	2	6	8	16	32	64	128	256	

(Although the third number in the last line should be "4," Joyce wrote "6.")

There was no place in the text, of course, for anything from the two groups quoted above, and they are not cancelled in the notes. Very occasionally, however, Joyce managed to make something of his equations, especially those not so baldly numerical. The entry "like × like = + unlike x," for example, is probably the source of the text's "common factors of similarity between their respective like and unlike reactions" (666). More certain is the relation of the following entries, on the left, to the text at the right:

$0 = 1/\text{many}$
$\infty = \text{many}/\text{one}$
$1 = 1/1$

From inexistence to existence he came to many and was as one received: existence with existence he was with any as any with any: from existence to nonexistence gone he would be by all as none perceived. (667–68)

multip × : prelim answer
merger in final fluxions
$= 17 \times 3(1 \ \& \ \text{carry} \ 2)$

...(every measure of reform or retrenchment being a preliminary solution to be contained by fluxion in the final solution)... (716)

cross × ation = nought

Reduce Bloom by cross multiplication...to a negligible negative irrational unreal quantity. (725)

A further point about such mathematical constructions: like thousands of others around the time of World War I, Joyce was attracted by the recently risen star of Bertrand Russell. While working on Ithaca, he read Russell's *Introduction to Mathematical Philosophy,* published in 1919, and immediately pressed the book into service. Phillip Herring has demonstrated that "more than fifty" of the Ithaca notes in the small Buffalo notebook were extracted from this work of Russell's (nothing from it appears in the British Museum notesheets).[22] After all, what could be more natural? Russell's very title could almost serve as a subtitle for Ithaca, and Joyce was not one to allow this opportunity to slip. He culled and converted. The first of the three mathematical conversions listed above is a fine example. Russell wrote, "It will be observed that zero and infinity, alone among ratios, are not one-one. Zero is one-many, and infinity is many-one" (65). There is Joyce's note, though even Russell may have frowned over its final application.

A frequent, and often justified, criticism of Joyce in his later work is that he just did not know when to stop, and so burdened his pages with too much of a good thing. His interminable catalogues, his long sections of stylistic experiment (such as the fifty-three-page "tired language" episode of Eumaeus—or, indeed, the seventy-two-page Ithacan catechism), his almost inhuman thoroughness in working into his text scores of rhetorical allusions here, hundreds of rivers there—all have drawn fire from critic and common reader alike. In short, Joyce is accused of not exercising sufficient selection. Thornton Wilder has put it neatly: "There is an obsessive compulsion toward the all-inclusive—what you might call the kitchen stove complex. He will get everything in there including the kitchen stove if he possibly can."[23] Wilder is speaking here of *Finnegans Wake,* but his remarks apply eminently to Ithaca—where, incidentally, the kitchen stove actually is included.

Joyce's use of the Ithaca notes suggests that although he may have had a compulsion toward the all-inclusive, it was less than obsessive. This is well summarized by his handling of the following two entries:

Bodes Law   (0 + 4) (3 + 4) (6 + 4) (12 + 4)
Kepler dist^3 = X of revol^2

In using these Joyce spares the reader the details of Bode's Law, but he retains those of Kepler's even though he must put them in verbal form: "the systematizations attempted by Bode and Kepler of cubes of distances and squares of times of revolution" (700). Sometimes he presents the gist of his figures, suppressing the actual numbers. In the kitchen, for example, Bloom decides not to lecture Stephen on "the respective percentage of protein and caloric energy in bacon, salt ling and butter, the absence of the former in the lastnamed and the abundance of the latter in the firstnamed" (673). The note is far more precise:

bacon 6d   9 protein grammes 7,295 caloric energy
salt cod 3½d 259   ---------   1,105   ---------

butter no protein
corn meal 1d 20,230 c. of en.

Although Joyce occasionally suppressed figures entirely ("1846 Jew dress act," "abs zero −273 C," "elm of Kildare 38 ft r" all appear in the book without the numbers), his usual practice was just what the reader of Ithaca would suspect: he used all the figures he possibly could. Dates, addresses and statistics are as prominent in the notes as they are in the text.

On other other hand there are the many notes Joyce rejected. Besides mathematical equations which simply could not be used, entries more germane to the episode were also rejected, and some could easily have produced whole questions. One can almost regret the neglect of such Leopoldian potentialities as these:

LB marked warm bits in book
LB 1 man on rolling platform
LB found grey hair in basin
LB mislays bad letter
LB finds mislaid book reconciliation

Or these concerning Stephen:

SD not in love∴trustable
X wd depopulate, SD starve all
SD objects to teach Molly Friday
SD thinking, thought flies to other (opposite)
SD−I live what I get

Other unused entries tease the imagination. One note proclaims, "Gynecocracy coming" (compare Molly's "I don't care what anybody says itd be much better for the world to be governed by the women in it" [778]), but another, surrounded by dreamhouse entries, reveals Bloom's idea of Woman's position: "possibility of back windows women in kitchen." And who knows what might have become of entries like "God a woman," "left hand = Mary of Magdalen," "find out you are in Dublin," or "If Earth got drunk!"?

Ithaca is funny, and as several entries have attested, so are some of its notes. Certainly the humor of the book's solemn description of Bloom's lofty urination—who "in his ultimate year at high school (1880) had been capable of attaining the point of greatest altitude against the whole concurrent strength of the institution, 210 scholars" (703)—is amply matched by its forthright source in the notes: "LB & boys pissed high." Bloom seated at his front-room table affords another example where the humor of the book's stilted pomposity is at least equaled by the laconic simplicity of a note: in the text Bloom "scratched imprecisely with his right hand, though insensible of prurition, various points and surfaces of his partly exposed, wholly abluted skin" (711), for which the note reads, "LB scratches all over without itch." One of the qualities Bloom admires in water is "its strength in rigid hydrants" (672); Joyce's note for this merely observes, in a mildly surprised tone, "How hard hydrants are." Humor at Molly's expense appears in a couple of entries: "LB up when she down & vice versa," and the intriguing "MB spasm old clockface." Just what Joyce had in mind in the latter note must remain a mystery, for it was not used.

At one point the humor is at Joyce's expense. Printed in a notesheet margin is the following:

```
ABCDEFGHIJKHLMNOPQRSTUVWXYZ
YXWVUTSRQPONMLKJIHGFEDCBA

ABC   DEF   GHI   JKL   MNOP   QRST   UVW   XYZ
ZYX   WVU   TSR   QPO   NMLK   JIHG   FED   CBA
```

The story is clear. Joyce was transposing the alphabet to work out Bloom's "reversed alphabetic" cipher concealing Martha Clifford's name and address (the same notesheet contains the entry, "LB etwas in cipher"). Working quickly, he set down the alphabet in regular order, but failed to see that he had included an extra "H"; he then began to reverse the alphabet underneath, and got as far as "Y" before realizing that he had more spaces to fill than letters available. With exaggerated care he began all over, this time grouping letters to insure accuracy, and completed the round trip safely.[24]

One page of the Ithaca notesheets differs from the rest in consisting almost entirely of references to events in the latter half of the *Odyssey*. All told, there are about sixty entries, with approximately half of them crossed out. Most of these notes, simply listing various actions of the Homeric characters, constitute little more than a kind of running plot-summary:

Tel sneezes. Pen laughs
Ul & Irus prizefight
Laer. kills Eupeithes, father of Antinous
Tel. forgets to lock armoury door
Melanthius is hanged up alive

Notes like these give the impression that Joyce, in recording them, wanted only a convenient prompter for his memory. Nevertheless, many of these "plot" entries have been crossed out, although they have apparently not been used in the novel, at least in any explicit sense.

Other Homeric notes on this page do more than record events, presenting as they do some sort of Joycean comment or interpretation:

    bow = long range gun
    Melanthius = Joe Cuffe
    Ul = W. Tell
    Ul beggar given inch takes all (jew gets own)
    UL = philosopher
    Ul. child of wrath: scar

Only the last three of these are crossed out; whether they were used in the book is not certain. Bloom does exhibit a scar on his hand in the Circe episode (563), and he is referred to as a philosopher in Ithaca (720). But he is hardly conspicuous for getting his own or taking all; Joyce may have "used" this entry in the ironic sense that this is just what Bloom does not do.

All in all, little is to be gained from a study of these Homeric references. Even the very few which establish definite Homeric connections within Ithaca do not, after all, increase the reader's understanding of the episode. When one discovers in the notes that "the Cat = Argos," or learns that Molly's cream represents ambrosia ("Ambrosia - cream"), no new insights are gained. Of much more importance in Ithaca than these Homeric correspondences are the cat as a Molly-symbol and Bloom's serving Molly's cream to Stephen. Litz, pointing out that Joyce made no use of many of the Homeric parallels, correctly assessed the real value of these notes: "...they illustrate how much more important the Homeric background was for Joyce than it is to the reader."[25]

So far, examination of the notes has been concerned with fairly large or comprehensive questions: Joyce's heavy reliance on them throughout all versions, the significance of the varied colors, the different types of notes and how they were used, and matters of science and selection, humor and Homer. It is time now to ask a question involving more restricted study of some of the entries: what can one learn from these notes about specific points or subjects in the final text?

The information provided by the notes is of several different kinds. One of these might be labeled "confirmation": a note confirms an interpretation which, to one degree or another, the text has already suggested. This sort of note states flatly a symbolic equation which Joyce has worked more or less equivocally into the final version. The importance of this is more than just a personal satisfaction in learning that, yes, Joyce did mean what one suspected in this or that passage. It goes a long way to vindicate the symbolist approach to Joyce, an approach which, over the years, has sometimes evoked some sharp critical controversy. The misguided, or unbridled, ingenuity of some zealous readers in interpreting Joyce symbolically has produced an understandable reaction, among other readers, against almost all such interpretation. Joyce's notes, however, unquestionably confirm the validity of a strongly symbolic interpretation, though of course they do not excuse or in any way justify unwarranted abuses of that approach.

A relatively elementary confirmation may perhaps best serve as an initial example of this sort of note. Throughout *Ulysses* much is made of "the promised land"; it lies behind Stephen's Parable of the Plums and Bloom's Agendath Netaim prospectus, and is closely connected with such motifs as Moses, fertility, and both exile and homecoming. When Bloom enters Molly's bed after his day of adventures, we are told that he experiences

> Satisfaction at the ubiquity in eastern and western terrestrial hemispheres, in all habitable lands and islands explored or unexplored (the land of the midnight sun, the islands of the blessed, the isles of Greece, the land of promise) of adipose posterior female hemispheres, redolent of milk and honey... (734)

And then he cautiously kisses "the plump mellow yellow smellow melons of her rump." Mention here of "the land of promise," together with the "milk and honey" of the Biblical description, makes it virtually certain that Joyce is equating Molly's rump, and Bloom's arrival thereat, with the promised land and Bloom's achievement thereof. Not much confirmation is required, but it is somehow gratifying nevertheless to find among the notes this entry: "Her rump = promised land."

Other confirmations are more important, involving passages where the text is less explicit. When Bloom and Stephen are looking at the stars, for example, they consider among many other astronomical phenomena "the interdependent gyrations of double suns," and "a new luminous sun generated by the collision and amalgamation in incandescence of two non-luminous exsuns" (700). The experienced Joycean is immediately alerted — surely this refers to Bloom and Stephen. The notes dispel any uncertainty: "SD & LB a double sun."

More ambiguous and controversial than these symbols, however, is the question of urination. That the subject held unusual fascination for Joyce we have confirmation in his work as a whole, from the play on the title of *Chamber Music* to many occasions in *Finnegans Wake*. And urine seems repeatedly, along with other liquids like water and tea, to invite association with such themes as fertility, creation, and fulfillment. This puzzling business, confused and elusive, not only resists proof or certainty, but even, by its very nature, tends to evoke a sense of the ridiculous. *Did* urine carry special meaning for Joyce? Do his notes provide any reassurance that symbolic interpretation here is not futile or even downright silly?

An entry in the Ithaca notesheets reads, "urine = sea, girls who longest, boys who highest." Only the last six words are crossed out since Joyce made explicit use of them (we have already examined "LB & boys pissed high"; as for "girls who longest," Molly remembers a time in the D.B.C. ladies' lavatory when "such a long one I did I forgot my suede gloves" [745]). The uncancelled status of "urine = sea" is not significant here; the fact remains that the idea was in Joyce's mind, and while this one equation certainly does not explain the whole complex problem, it does reinforce serious inquiry.

Another kind of informative note, instead of confirming some point, increases understanding and appreciation either by presenting something new or by calling attention to something easily overlooked. A note like "MB more given to lilt if LB dumpy," for example, cancelled but without explicit statement in the text, summarizes succinctly an impression implicitly present through much of the book. Again, although many passages in the text show that artistic Stephen is superstitious while scientific Bloom is not, a note reveals that Joyce also associated superstition with race: "SD (aryan) superstit. (LB) semitic not." An example of information entirely suppressed in the text concerns Milly and her photograph. Bloom remembers that "on the duke's lawn entreated by an English visitor, she declined to permit him to make and take away her photographic image (objection not stated)" (693). Joyce may have omitted Molly's objection in order to allow the England-versus-Ireland symbolism here freer play, but a note tells us that Molly, dominantly semitic though she is, is superstitious: "Molly feared her photo part of self." For a final example there is the business of parallax. This astronomical term plagues Bloom off and on throughout the day: He cannot recall just what it means or how it operates, and apparently goes to bed with this minor problem unsolved. Actually, he does recall what parallax is — not only recalls it but explains it to Stephen. To perceive this requires careful reading. Sandwiched among the catalogue of astronomical phenomena which Bloom rehearses with Stephen in his back yard is this inconspicuous item: "the parallax or parallactic drift of socalled fixed stars" (698). Even the close reader is likely to miss the point of this, simply noting that "parallax" has popped up again — as it happens, for the last time. But among the Ithaca notes is "Parallax? he remembers." Bloom has come through, and parallax joins Archimedes, Moses without candle, and the battle of Plevna as a solved problem.

A last kind of informative note presents meanings or relationships entirely absent from the final text and known to Joyce only. These provide some insight into the complex associational working of Joyce's mind, the mind which saw signatures in all things, but often, even with the notes, one is left little wiser than before. A note like the following causes no trouble: "men less longlived after flood (damp = death)." This was used for part of the question, "What relation existed between their ages?" where Joyce mentions "the maximum postdiluvian age of 70" as opposed to "the maximum antediluvian age, that of Methusalah, 969 years" (679). Joyce, probably in a mythical sense, attributed man's shortened life to the dampness introduced by the flood. This is mildly interesting and plain enough; no difficulties ensue. Other notes are not so simple. "Desire = hidden identity," for example, would seem to be as abstruse as it is abstract. Was it used for "the statue of Narcissus, sound without echo, desired desire" (728), and does the "hidden identity" refer to Stephen? More likely it concerns the "concealed identities" Bloom and Stephen see in each other (689), and carries an allusion to Aristophanes' speech in Plato's *Symposium,* where he maintains that originally mankind had four legs and four arms, until, alarmed at their power, Zeus bisected them; ever since then the severed halves search for their counterparts, and love is (in Jowett's translation) "the desire of one another which is implanted in us, reuniting our original nature, making one of two, and healing the state of man."

A similar problem, not quite so ambiguous since the note can be traced definitely to the text, is posed by "LB in tree (jew)." In his youth Bloom "had climbed up into a secure position amid the ramifications of a tree on Northumberland road to see the entrance (2 February 1888) into the capital of a demonstrative torchlight procession" (716–17). But the text gives no indication, as the note does, that Bloom's climbing a tree is to be associated with his Jewishness. (Two other notes refer to this event without mention of race: "LB in tree to see entry" and "LB climbed along branch"; the latter note is uncancelled.) There may be an allusion here to the publican who climbed a tree to see Christ's passage through Jericho (Luke 19:4), but if so, this hardly explains the tree-jew connection of Joyce's note. Did Joyce simply associate climbing with the proverbial Hebraic characteristics of initiative and opportunism? The note must remain a mystery.

This examination of Joyce's notes has been confined to some twenty pages for the Ithaca episode. When one realizes that for other episodes about ninety more pages, in the British Museum notesheets and the small Buffalo notebook, still await close study, the possibilities of gaining new knowledge of Joyce's mind and art become pressingly apparent. But here and now attention belongs on the *raison d'être* of the Ithaca notes—the actual composition of the episode in manuscript, typescript and proof.

3

The Building of Ithaca

Method and Materials

By the time an author has collected and arranged notes, struggled through the writing of rough drafts, and made a fair copy, creative labor is usually nearly or entirely done. For Joyce, completion of the fair copy was just a good beginning. After finishing the basic version of an episode, he adopted what may be called an accretive method of composition. Each successive version became a new foundation on which to erect additional superstructure. The virgin margins of copybooks, typescript pages, and proofsheets were irresistible invitations to violation. Little was changed, still less was deleted; additions, flowering from seeds in the notes, filled those margins. Although Joyce followed this process in both manuscript and typescript, the proofsheets have attracted the most notice, mainly because proofsheets are usually a means of typographical correction, not, as with Joyce, a challenge to further composition. Ellmann put it this way: "With Joyce, the reading of proofs was a creative act; he insisted on five sets, and made innumerable changes, almost always additions, in the text."[1] And Sylvia Beach announced, "Joyce told me that he had written a third of *Ulysses* on the proofs."[2]

The accretive method is feasible only to the extent that an author is very sure that additions are just as they should be; otherwise the text would soon become an impossible nightmare of cancellations, substitutions, and re-additions. Joyce's certainty in this respect was nothing short of awesome; he would occasionally cancel a word or two, or substitute a short phrase, but the great majority of his additions went down without a blot and remained untampered with from then on. Selection, arrangement and revision took place in Joyce's mind; the written addition simply recorded the result. Frank Budgen has emphasized this: "Joyce's method of composition always seemed to me to be that of a poet rather than that of a prose writer. The words he wrote were far advanced in his mind before they found shape on paper."[3]

Once embarked on this accretive process Joyce was never sure where he would end up—or when. He was forever underestimating the time it would take him to finish a particular episode or, for that matter, the book itself. At one point he hoped to complete the book in the fall of 1921. Instead, he spent that fall surrounded by proofs, furiously adding to them. Episodes steadily accumulated material until they became far longer than originally foreseen. Early in 1921, for example, he wrote to Harriet Weaver that he hoped to finish Eumaeus soon, saying, "This will leave me the time I need for composing the two final and shorter episodes."[4] Actually, of course, both Ithaca and Penelope are longer than Eumaeus.

What does the accretive method mean as far as Ithaca is concerned? It means that Joyce, after completing the basic draft and making a fair copy, worked through the episode from beginning to end six different times, incorporating a new set of additions each time. These six versions are the manuscript, first and second typescript, first and second galley proof, and the final page proof. The following table shows the number and percentage of words that each stage contributed to the total text:

	Words	Percentage of whole
Basic manuscript	13,041	58%
Additions to:		
Manuscript	1,771	8%
First typescript	3,638	16%
Second typescript	725	3%
First galley proof	1,106	5%
Second galley proof	1,259	6%
Page proof	881	4%
Total	22,421	100%

Joyce thus added 9,380 words, or 42 percent of the episode, after making the fair copy of the basic manuscript. He changed only 348. He deleted entirely an almost negligible 79.

Before examining in detail the additions Joyce made throughout these six versions of Ithaca, we need a better idea of the materials themselves. What do the manuscript, typescript, and proofs look like, and how did Joyce operate when working with them?

The manuscript, housed in the Rosenbach Foundation in Philadelphia, is the basic fair copy of *Ulysses*.[5] Although the earlier episodes are "clean" in that they contain little or no marginal addition, the later episodes, festooned with additions, are a combination of fair copy and working draft. In the manuscript, then, Ithaca really displays two stages of composition, the basic fair copy made from the missing rough draft, and the numerous additions subsequently made as Joyce, beginning the long process of accretion, overhauled the fair copy.

The manuscript is contained in two notebooks labeled "Ithaca I" and "Ithaca II." Following his usual practice, Joyce filled the right-hand pages with the basic text or fair copy, leaving the left-hand pages clear for revision. He numbered only the right-hand pages, thirty-two in notebook I and twenty-one in notebook II. The basic manuscript contains 226 of Ithaca's final total of 309 questions and answers; twenty-four new questions were added in the left-hand pages, plus of course much new material to expand the original questions.

The arrangement of the text in the two notebooks is unusual and significant, since it clearly reveals the pressure of time under which Joyce was working. The text falls into five large sections, apportioned three to notebook I and two to notebook II, as follows (using the pagination of Ithaca, 666–737, in the Modern Library edition):

Notebook I	Notebook II
666–681	681–692
692–705	705–720
720–737	

In composing the episodes, Joyce thus shifted back and forth between the two notebooks. The purpose of this seems at first to be obscure, but is confirmed by the evidence of the typescript: Ithaca was typed while it was being written, and Joyce simply alternated between the two notebooks so that he could continue composition in one while the other was at the typist's. The numbering of the typescript pages makes this certain. The typist numbered each new batch of pages beginning with "1," so that it is easily possible to see where each separate batch begins and ends. And the beginning and end of each notebook section tallies precisely with the beginning or end of a batch of typescript. Later Joyce renumbered the typed pages in proper sequence.

For many years any student of the textual evolution of *Ulysses* was stopped cold at the typescript stage. Slocum and Cahoon's *Bibliography* included this chilling information: "Sylvia Beach in her catalogue of 1935, item No. 6, lists: 'A selection of typescript pages with autograph corrections by the Author, from 5 to 15 lines per page. These pages may be acquired separately by those who might like to enrich their copy of "Ulysses" with a little manuscript of Joyce.'" And the bibliographers close their section on *Ulysses* manuscripts with the observation that "The above typescript pages and odds and ends of proof are without doubt scattered all over Europe and America."[6]

In 1959, however, the University of Buffalo was fortunate enough to acquire from Miss Beach most of the Joyce materials still in her possession, including more than 700 pages of *Ulysses* typescript.[7] For Ithaca there are fifty-four pages of original, or first, typescript, thirty-four pages of the second and two pages of the third. There are also two pages containing only autograph additions. As accurately as can be judged, these Ithaca holdings are approximately 70 percent complete.

With the first typescript it is of course easy to tell what is missing (twenty-one pages), but it is impossible to be so precise with the second and third typescripts. As noted earlier, when Joyce's additions to an original page were slight, it went to the printer without being retyped. Other pages, more heavily laden, went back to the typist, sometimes twice. But it is not always possible to be sure, with some pages, whether a second or third typescript was actually made. Two tests can be applied in these cases. First, of course, the original page can be compared with the first galley proof; if the proof contains material not present in the typed page, then at least one intervening typescript becomes certain. The second test, less reliable, is the "smudge" test: a page displaying inky smudges from printers' fingers is obviously terminal. Since many pages, however, are identical in text with the proof yet are unsmudged, often a page was retyped and sent to the printer without further additions, leaving behind the unsmudged original. In these cases it is doubtful that Joyce even saw the retyped copy: it would certainly have received more additions. Instead, it probably went directly from the typist to Miss Beach and then to the printer. This was almost certainly the case with all pages which got as far as a third typescript, for Joyce never made additions to these.

Reconstruction of material added to a missing page, provided there is at least one copy, first or second, is of course a simple matter of collation with the preceding Rosenbach manuscript or the following galley proof. Where sections of the typescript are entirely missing, however, collation may reveal what has been added but not when it was added: there is no way of knowing how many typescript versions existed. Even here, though, help often comes from Joyce's old notebook habit of making additions on the blank left-hand pages. He followed a similar system with the typescript also, writing an addition to a page on the back of the preceding page. Thus even though a page is missing one can tell, from the extant preceding page, that a particular addition belongs to the first or second typescript.

In contrast to the problems presented by manuscript and typescript, the proofs of Ithaca are clear and simple. The two sets of galley proofs, in

Harvard's Houghton Library, are complete.[8] As mentioned earlier, each set consists of eight large sheets or placards; those of Ithaca are numbered from 6 to 13, with the Eumaeus episode absorbing the first five. Each placard except the last, which runs to only half a sheet, contains eight blocks or pages of type, slightly larger than the page sizes of either the Shakespeare or Modern Library editions. (There are sixty page-blocks in the proof, but seventy and seventy-two pages in the Shakespeare and Modern Library editions respectively.) Eight of the placards, when pulled, were dated by the printer:

Placard	Proof 1	Proof 2
6	15 December 1921	29 December 1921
7	16 December 1921	30 December 1921
8	17 December 1921	
9	21 December 1921	2 January 1922
11		5 January 1922

These dates carry their own tale of what the Christmas season of 1921 must have been like for Joyce—and probably for his family as well. One recalls the Christmas card in Bloom's desk drawer: "May this Yuletide bring to thee, Joy and peace and welcome glee" (720). It brought Joyce, almost daily, garbled proofs.

The page proofs, in the Humanities Research Center of the University of Texas, have been cut up into single pages, but when Joyce and the printers worked with them they were large sheets containing sixteen pages each, eight to a side.[9] As each sheet was corrected, it was marked "*bon à tirer*" and signed by both Joyce and Sylvia Beach. Only the second of the five Ithaca sheets was dated by the printer when the proofs were pulled—January 19, 1922; but all five were dated at the printer's when they were returned corrected, the first two on January 25 and the last three on January 27.

Changes

The changes Joyce made in words already written—relatively few, affecting only several hundred words—provide small "before and after" pictures of portions of the text. It is often easier to see Joyce's purpose in substituting one word for another than it is to understand the reason for a newly created addition.

The great majority of revisions are as brief as they are infrequent. One or two words are substituted for one or two others. In a few places, however, revision is more extensive, and most of these longer changes occur not in the answer passages but in the questions themselves. Joyce added to the answers and occasionally changed a word here and there, but he found it necessary to rewrite entirely some questions. The answers deal with facts; they concern concrete objects, precise statistics, definite actions or events. Joyce could easily make them as involved, as "Ithacan," as he wished, simply by adding more and still more facts. But the questions posed a problem: since by nature they rarely contained factual information, their complexity had to be evolved through language and style. Frequently, therefore, Joyce would completely recast a simple question to invest it with suitable rhetorical pomposity. In the following examples, the original question is followed by the revised version:

What did Bloom think that Stephen thought about Bloom?

What, reduced to their simplest reciprocal form, were Bloom's thoughts about Stephen's thoughts about Bloom and Bloom's thoughts about Stephen's thoughts about Bloom's thoughts about Stephen? (682)

Why did he not conclude?

Why was the chant arrested at the conclusion of this first distich? (689)

Was it possible to contract for these several schemes?

Positing what protasis would the contraction for such several schemes become a natural and necessary apodosis? (719)

From what reverse of fortune did these supports protect their possessor?

Reduce Bloom by cross multiplication of reverses of fortune, from which these supports protected him, and by elimination of all positive values to a negligible negative irrational unreal quantity. (725)

Most revisions, however, involve only single words or short phrases. One change Joyce made again and again was to replace simple words with more formal, polysyllabic synonyms. In some of his most jargonistic substitutions, "they speak" becomes "the duumvirate deliberate," "mental occupations" becomes "syllabus of intellectual pursuits," and "a bowl of" becomes "a cylindrical canister containing." The following changes, only a sampling, suggest Joyce's continual search for *le mot gros*:

put - inserted	start - initiation
get - obtain	streets - public thoroughfares
sun - solar disk	entered - gained retarded access
give - adduce	words - polysyllables
meal -collation	prepared - decocted

Less frequently, Joyce would change a word to achieve more precise or appropriate expression. Thus "a few seconds" becomes "ten seconds"; "shocked by the impact" becomes "concussed by the impact"; and "Stephen's breakdown" becomes "Stephen's collapse." A brilliantly successful example appears as Joyce describes the stars moving "from immeasurably remote eons to infinitely remote futures in comparison with which the years, threescore and ten, of allotted human life formed a period of infinitesimal brevity" (698). In the revision, the closing phrase becomes "a parenthesis of infinitesimal brevity"; the improvement is evident.

Joyce's insistence on absolute accuracy in names, addresses, and statistics is well known, but it is nevertheless impressing to observe the care he exercised on this fidelity to fact, for many of his changes were made for the sake of accuracy. Sirius, at first nine lightyears away, is later placed at a more nearly correct ten lightyears (698). The atmospheric pressure the human body can sustain is given as sixteen tons, then changed to nineteen tons (699). Hozier's *History of the Russo-Turkish War,* in Bloom's library, was first listed as written by Hardiman. The address of the Gaiety Theatre is several times given as South Anne Street, later not only corrected to South King Street, but pinpointed as 46, 47, 48, 49 South King Street. "Leeson street bridge" becomes "Eustace bridge, upper Leeson street" (671). And "Viscount Ripon," whose torchlight procession in 1888 Bloom climbed a tree to watch, is changed to "the marquess of Ripon" (717): Ripon, who enjoyed the courtesy title of viscount in early life, had been a marquess for many years by 1888.[10]

Still another purpose of revision is wordplay. Here is one of the major sources of humor in Ithaca, yet because of its hidden and frequently subtle nature, it often goes unnoticed by not only the ordinary reader but experienced critic as well. Anyone, of course, after reading only two or three pages of Ithaca is aware that Joyce is playing with words for balance, antithesis, circumlocution, scientific jargon, and so on. But another kind of wordplay permeates the episode—the kind involving hidden meanings, puns, disguised redundancies, and Latin etymologies. It seldom occurs to the reader to look for such sparkling, loaded words in a section where language appears to be just the opposite—exact, objective, cold. One does not, after all, expect linguistic horseplay in a scientific report.

Here is the sort of thing that should warn readers to watch the vocabulary of Ithaca very carefully. In the manuscript, Mrs. Riordan studies passersby through Bloom's "onelensed fieldglasses." To this, in galley proof, Joyce added one word, and the phrase became "onelensed binocular fieldglasses" (680). The ridiculous linguistic clash here is not hard to catch, but other examples are less apparent. William York Tindall said, "It is worth-while looking everything in Joyce up," and a desk dictionary will often serve the purpose. With it, for example, one learns that Bloom's books display "scintillating titles" (708) not merely because they sparkle in the candlelight, or because their contents, ironically, are anything but sparkling, but also because "scintillating" is a technical term in astronomy, referring to the twinkling of stars. Another example, and one of the funniest, appears in an addition to a galley proof. The extraordinary altitude of Bloom's urination, we are told, is nothing unusual for the expert who in high school could outperform "the whole strength of the institution, 210 scholars." Then, with nothing short of positive inspiration, Joyce revised it to "the whole *concurrent* strength" (703). A little high school Latin, awareness of context, and any sense of humor are all the reader needs—once he notices the word to begin with.

So far, these examples of wordplay have not involved substitution of one word for another— *binocular* and *concurrent* are additions, and *scintillating* is present in manuscript. It is far more instructive to watch Joyce replace one word with another to achieve hidden meanings. Molly's lighted window provides a striking double example. Standing in the darkness of the garden, Bloom calls Stephen's attention to the light above them (702). At this point the manuscript reads:

> How did he elucidate the mystery of an invisible person, his wife Marion (Molly) Bloom, indicated by a visible vigilant luminous sign, a lamp?

There is already at least one highly charged word here: with *elucidate,* Bloom throws light on light. But Joyce returned three times to this passage for revision. In the first typescript, he merely cancels *luminous,* since he had already used it in the preceding question. In the second typescript, though, he changed *indicated* to *denoted,* creating the redundancy *denoted by a . . . sign.* Finally, in the second galley proof, he changes *vigilant* to *splendid* (L. *splendere,* to shine). Loaded words like these are not easily noticeable, and are often overlooked, but when tripped over they explode like hidden landmines.

Joyce repeatedly makes changes to produce this sort of wordplay. The manuscript tells us that Bloom in his kitchen "carried the iron kettle to the tap and sink in order to draw water." This is later changed to "carried the iron kettle to the sink to tap the current" (670), with the resulting pun on "tap." As a child Milly had "a doll, a boy, a sailor she threw away"; the last words are changed, appropriately for a sailor, to "cast away" (693). At first Bloom puts out his candle "by a sharp ejection of breath upon its flame," but an airy redundancy appears when "ejection" is changed to "expiration" (669).

The olives in the kitchen cupboard (675) provide one of Joyce's cleverest hidden redundancies, based again, as many of them are, upon Latin roots. An entry in the British Museum notesheets reads, "Oily paper (of olives)," and the manuscript lists among the contents of the shelves "four black olives in oily paper." Joyce was tickled by the derivation of "oily" from the Latin *oleum,* one of whose meanings is olive-oil. In the first typescript he takes this one step further, and replaces "oily" with "oleaginous" (L. *olea,* olive). Not only has he gained a bigger word, but the phrase is now twice as redundant, reading, in effect, "black olives in oily olive-ish paper."

One last example of wordplay is not a pun or etymological redundancy, but a typically Joycean brand of impishness — so Joycean, in fact, that it has been mistakenly removed in later editions as a misprint. With an addition to the final page proof Joyce expanded the phrase "a book entitled *Sweets of Sin*" to "a book of inferior literary style, entitled *Sweets of Sin*" (688). At the same time, he crossed out "entitled" and substituted "entituled." A later editor or printer, however, familiar with English orthography but not with Irish humor, failed to appreciate this shift to inferiority, and "corrected" the supposed misprint. So the matter stands, regrettably, in the Modern Library edition.

Additions

The additions made to Ithaca throughout six different drafts almost hide the forest in the trees. Responsible for 42 percent of the episode, these additions range all the way from single words to as many as five consecutive new questions. The very profusion of this material makes its classification and analysis difficult. As with Bloom and his infinite number, the 9th power of the 9th power of 9, so with Joyce and his additions: "the nucleus of the nebula of every digit of every series containing succinctly the potentiality of being raised to the utmost kinetic elaboration of any power of any of its powers" (699).

On the other hand, Joyce's accretive method, by its very nature, prompts an observation which may provide a start: Joyce added much of his material because he simply wanted *more.* Obvious as this sounds, it can easily be forgotten. With so cunning and complex a writer as Joyce, a very real danger lies in attempting to discover some clever purpose behind this or that addition, when actually the vast majority originate in what Thornton Wilder called Joyce's "obsessive compulsion toward the all-inclusive," or "the kitchen-stove complex." This is not to say, of course, that subtleties and complexities are not there, or that additions were never made for purposes of theme or symbolism or style. But it is to say that Joyce, especially in the concretely factual episode of Ithaca, was primarily concerned with the need for expansion. Indeed, such addition in Ithaca becomes its own justification, for an almost stupefying mass of factual detail is, in itself, one of the episode's major purposes. Catalogues and itemization, subdivision and multiplication, *things* and *things* and *things* — these are the life cells of Ithaca.

With this in mind, we may perhaps best begin by considering the addition of entire questions. More than a quarter of Ithaca's questions (83 out of 309) were added after the basic manuscript was written, appearing in the various drafts as follows:

Manuscript additions	24
First typescript	31
Second typescript	2
First galley proof	4
Second galley proof	14
Page proof	8

Except for a minor splurge in the second galley proof, Joyce had completed the formulation of most of his questions — and the essential structure of the episode — by the end of the first typescript. Those added to the last four stages are usually short, often supplying transition or clarification.

Relatively few of the eighty-three added questions introduce wholly new subjects or actions. Except for passages describing Molly's handkerchiefs hanging in the kitchen and Bloom's subsequent urge to give one to Stephen (670,677), Bloom's reactions to the torn betting tickets (675–76), Mrs. Sinico's death and Mrs. Dedalus' funeral (695), the compilation of the budget (711) and the three "enigmas" Bloom contemplates as he prepares for bed (the loud crack from the table, the identity of M'Intosh, and the whereabouts of Moses "when the candle went out" (729) — except for these passages (totaling fourteen questions) most of the new questions expand or elaborate upon material already present. Four are added, for example, to the dreamhouse section, each cataloguing still further possibilities for the grounds or Bloom's country-gentleman pursuits. Again, after Bloom has feasted on his delicious concoction of get-rich-quick schemes, Joyce serves him dessert with an added question on finding a goldmine (719). And when Bloom, entering the bedroom, is struck by Molly's resemblance to her father, Major Tweedy, an addition presents his recollection of the major arriving and departing by train (730).

Some of the new questions, however, serve more functional purposes. Occasionally a smoother transition is desirable. In the basic manuscript, for example, after the episode opens by tracing Bloom and Stephen's course through the streets, the second question asks, "What action did Bloom make on their arrival at their destination?" (the ninth question in the final text). The strolling pair have reached Eccles Street far too suddenly, and consequently Joyce adds to the manuscript five questions, placed between the above two, in which, still walking, they discuss all sorts of subjects. Another rough transition occurs in the manuscript when Bloom reenters the house after bidding farewell to Stephen. He is in the garden when a question abruptly asks, "What suddenly arrested his ingress?" and we learn he has bumped his head on a walnut sideboard in the front room. But again this is moving too fast from one place to another, and Joyce adds to the first typescript the question which carefully takes Bloom every step of the way:

> Did he remain?
>
> With deep inspiration he returned, retraversing the garden, reentering the passage, reclosing the door. With brief suspiration he reassumed the candle, reascended the stairs, reapproached the door of the front room, hallfloor, and reentered. (705)

Now Bloom, and the reader as well, is ready for that walnut sideboard.

Clarification is also a reason for new questions. It is most revealing, in an episode which no one denies is often difficult in both form and content, to watch Joyce work very carefully to eliminate confusion and prevent possible misunderstanding. Some of the critics who have accused him of willful obscurity, hoax or downright dementia should spend a few hours with his manuscripts. A good example of addition for clarity occurs after Stephen narrates his Queen's Hotel epiphany (684). The text at this point asks, "What suggested scene was then reconstructed by Bloom?" and the answer describes the details of his father's suicide. Later, however, Joyce realized that the reader was likely to assume here that Bloom actually tells Stephen about the suicide. Bloom may be in a confiding mood, but it does not extend this far, and so a manuscript addition asks, "Did he depict the scene verbally for his guest to see?" The answer makes it clear he did not. (The redundant wordplay of "depict...verbally...to see" is typical.)

In another passage Joyce added a clarifying question, still was not satisfied, and so later added a second. After the catalogue of Bloom's books, the manuscript poses the question:

Why, firstly and secondly, did he not consult the work in question?

Firstly, in order to exercise mnemotechnic: secondly, because after an interval of amnesia, when seated at the central table, about to consult the work in question, he remembered by mnemotechnic the name of the military engagement, Plevna. (710)

This is far too cryptic. The "work in question" has not been identified, and even if an astute reader deduces, from "Plevna" and the preceding catalogue, that the work must be the *History of the Russo-Turkish War,* the humor of the passage is blocked by its ambiguity. In the second galley proof, accordingly, Joyce preceded the question with this addition:

Which volume was the largest in bulk?
Hozier's *History of the Russo-Turkish War.* .

But this still leaves room for temporary doubt: is this bulkiest volume the "work in question" which Bloom does not consult for "Plevna"? A second addition, in the final proof, appears between the two questions and removes all confusion:

What among other data did the second volume of the work in question contain?

The name of a decisive battle (forgotten), frequently remembered by a decisive officer, major Brian Cooper Tweedy (remembered).

The text now moves through a clear sequence: Hozier, work in question, decisive battle (forgotten), did not consult, remembered, Plevna.

In one clarifying addition, concerning the two chairs in Bloom's front room (706), Joyce does something very rare in his work: he calls explicit attention to his symbolism. As the position, shape, color and material of the two chairs are described in detail, the reader need be no Joycean expert to realize that the "squat stuffed easychair with stout arms extended and back slanted to the rere" and the "slender splayfoot chair of glossy cane curves" are caricatures of buxom, sensual Molly and youthful, sprightly Milly (or, possibly, flashy Blazes Boylan). But Joyce takes no chances. Immediately following, in the manuscript, he adds this question:

What significances attached to these two chairs?

Significances of similitude, of posture, of symbolism, of circumstantial evidence, of testimonial supermanence.

Some of Joyce's added questions intensify the elaborate balance of parallelism and antithesis that is so prominent a feature of Ithaca's style.

After the question, "What did Stephen see on raising his gaze to the height of a yard from the fire towards the opposite wall?" Joyce inserts, "What did Bloom see on the range?" (670) Again, just before the question, "What caused him irritation in his sitting posture?" appears the addition, "What caused him consolation in his sitting posture?" (710) One of the episode's most striking passages originates in this way. In the garden with Stephen, Bloom indulges in "Meditations of evolution increasingly vaster," including the milky way, solar system and fixed stars (698). By itself this question presents a fine telescopic, macrocosmic view of man in his universe. Joyce later intensifies this, however, by reversing his field, so to speak, and inserting a question which presents the microscopic, microcosmic view: "Were there obverse meditations of involution increasingly less vast?" Here we are led "inwards" through rock formations, bacteria and molecular structure.

We may conclude and summarize the examination of questions added for transition, clarity, and balance by noting an addition where all three of these purposes are present. In the manuscript there is nothing about Bloom's farewell to Stephen and the latter's departure. Instead, immediately after they urinate beneath Molly's window the text continues:

> Alone, what did Bloom feel?
>
> The cold of interstellar space, thousands of degrees below freezing point or the absolute zero of Fahrenheit, Centigrade or Réaumur: the incipient intimations of proximate dawn. (704)

Stephen has been dismissed with confusing suddenness, and the reader gropes for orientation. The following question, added just before the one above, provides transition to the solitary Bloom, clarifies the fact of Stephen's departure, and balances the phrasing of the manuscript:

> Alone, what did Bloom hear?
>
> The double reverberation of retreating feet on the heavenborn earth, the double vibration of a jew's harp in the resonant lane.

Later Joyce added a further half-dozen questions here with more explicit details of the farewell—the opening of the gate, the valedictory handshake, and the chiming of the church bells.

Mention, in the last example, of Stephen's "retreating feet" (exile) and "a jew's harp" (Bloom's influence on artistic Stephen?) brings up another function of many additions—symbolism. This involves not only whole questions, of course, but shorter elements as well, right down to single

words. Examination of symbolic additions, however, will have to be restricted in two ways. First, since almost everything in *Ulysses* is, or can be
suspected of being, symbolic, any survey must necessarily be highly selec-
tive. Secondly, the present study of Ithaca's textual evolution is no place
for analysis or interpretation of symbolism—that belongs, and will appear,
in Part Two, devoted to a critical study of the episode in its final form.

Much of Ithaca's symbolism is present in the basic manuscript, but
Joyce seized every opportunity, in his revision, to intensify and increase his
symbols. Sometimes this prompted the addition of entire questions. The
highly charged passages describing Bloom and Stephen's ceremonial
procession from the house (697–98), the meteor streaking "from Vega in
the Lyre...towards the zodiacal sign of Leo" (703), the statue of Narcissus
(710), and Bloom as Everyman and Noman (727) all appear as added questions. At other times Joyce made a relatively short addition within a
question, and his symbolism was less than profound. One such passage
presents humorous symbols very like the two chairs noted earlier, but in
this case the Molly-Milly surrogates are two onions in the kitchen dresser.
Actually this example might be classified as a change instead of an addition, but since Joyce's revision turned an insignificant three-word phrase
into a symbolic eighteen-word passage, far more was added than changed.
The manuscript catalogue of that dresser includes "a bisected onion."
Later this becomes "two onions, one the larger, Spanish, entire, the other,
smaller, Irish, bisected with augmented surface and more redolent" (675).

One of the major purposes of Ithaca's symbolism is to present Bloom
and Stephen in a relationship of unity, equality, or even consubstantiality,
and many of Joyce's symbolic additions emphasize this theme. The significant word "parallel" in the opening words of the episode ("What parallel
course did Bloom and Stephen follow returning?" [666]) is an addition, as
are the equally significant words beginning this question's answer:
"Starting united..." The symbolic spoonerism, "Stoom...Blephen," in the
question where each is "substituting" for the other (682), is a last-minute
page proof addition (the word "substituting" itself is an earlier addition).
The communion symbolism associated with drinking the cocoa also
provides examples. "Relinquishing his symposiarchal right to the mustache
cup," Bloom drinks from "a cup identical with that of his guest" (677). The
word "symposiarchal" is an addition: Bloom is not, at this point, in a
position of symposiarchal authority, but is identical with Stephen.
Wordplay is also a purpose here: the term comes from *syn-posis,* "a
drinking together." And in the next question the eucharistic words "Epp's
massproduct, the creature cocoa" are additions to the final proof.

Symbolism aside, the myriad of other words and phrases added to
Ithaca serve several purposes besides the ever-dominant attempt to pile up

more and still more data. For one thing, Joyce, like any artist, strove constantly for specific detail, and in an episode like Ithaca, where the particular serves both as a gateway to the universal and archetypal and simultaneously as an end in itself—facts for facts' sake—the addition of detail became a positive obsession. The examples below, with the added words italicized, are only drops in the brimming bucket of Ithaca's details:

two *spoonseat deal* chairs (669)
the man's back and *listed feet and lighted* candle (669)
lemonflavoured soap, *to which paper still adhered* (672-73)
a jug *of brown crockery* (675)
good working *solidungular* cob (*roan gelding, 14h*) (714)
garden boots *with elastic gussets* (714)
decomposed vegetable missles (726)
the *indexfinger and thumb of the* right hand (737)

Another kind of addition sharpened setting and mood by specifying weather, time of day, or season of year:

in the coffeeroom of Breslin's hotel *on a rainy Sunday in the January of 1892* (680)
He had sometimes propelled her *on warm summer evenings* (680)
Rudolph Bloom (Rudolph Virag) died on *the evening of* the 27 June 1886 (684) once in *the summer of* 1898 (696)

Finally, there are those words and phrases Joyce collected in his notes for use whenever suitable. Many of these, of course, are scientific terms, inserted here and there throughout the different drafts: "common factors" (666), "like and unlike" (666), "integral parts" (697), and "working hypothesis" (700). Sometimes Joyce would add an adjective, decide later that it would serve better somewhere else, and so shift it to a new position. The pair "ipsorelative" and "aliorelative," for example, first appear in the added question about Bloom's goldmine (first typescript):

What eventually would render him independent of such aliorelative wealth?

The independent discovery of an ipsorelative goldseam of inexhaustible ore.

But the second typescript brought second thoughts, and Joyce shifted the two words to the description of Bloom's reflection in the mirror: "The image of a solitary (ipsorelative) mutable (aliorelative) man" (708).

Nothing is more fascinating about Joyce's additions than the way he gradually built up some of his long catalogues. The three longest questions in Ithaca consist of such catalogues: the specifications of Bloom's dreamhouse (548 words), the contents of his first table drawer (538 words), and the qualities he admires in water (476 words). The table-drawer question received thorough attention at an early stage: it is 82 percent complete in the basic manuscript. The other two Joyce "made up" as he went along, adding more details in every draft (approximately three-quarters of each question was added after the basic manuscript).

The "water hymn," by far the most complex and interesting of these questions, is worth examining in detail. Because of the extraordinary pains Joyce took here, it is possible to separate his additions into no fewer than eight different stages: two typescripts, two galley proofs, the page proof, and three groups of manuscript additions. The last of these requires explanation. In making his additions to this question in the manuscript notebook, Joyce not only added directly to the basic text, but also added to his additions and, at one point, added to an addition to an addition. The notebook pages became laced with a concatenation of lines as Joyce would draw a line from text to margin, write an addition, then draw another line from this addition to the blank left-hand page, write another addition, and finally draw a third line from there to another part of the page and write a third addition. Thus, like boxes fitting inside each other, third fits into second, second into first, and first into basic text.

The following table presents a statistical summary of the part each draft played in the evolution of this question. Note that the 109 words of the basic manuscript represent only 23 percent of the final version. Additions account for the remaining 77 percent.

	Words	Percentage of whole
Basic manuscript	109	23%
Additions to:		
1. Manuscript text directly	52	11%
2. Additions	106	22%
3. An addition to an addition	4	1%
4. First typescript	54	11%
5. Second typescript	79	17%
6. First galley proof	9	2%
7. Second galley proof	5	1%
8. Page proof	58	12%
	476	100%

The best way to appreciate fully the remarkable nature of this piecemeal construction is to see the entire question set down in such a way that every word can be traced to the draft in which it first appeared. An attempt to do this is made below. In this reconstruction, only the words not italicized are present in the basic manuscript. All italicized words were added later, and the raised numbers indicate at which of the eight stages, listed above, the preceding words were added. Words crossed out were replaced by the following italics in whatever stage the numerals indicate.

What in water did Bloom, ~~carrying water~~, *waterlover, drawer of water, watercarrier* [6] returning to the range, admire?

Its universality: its *democratic* [5] equality and constancy to its nature in seeking its own level: its vastness in the ocean of Mercator's ~~projector~~ *projection:* [8] *its unplumbed profundity in the Sundam trench of the Pacific exceeding 8,000 fathoms:* [1] *the restlessness of its waves and surface particles visiting in turn all points of its seaboard:* [2] *the independence of its units:* [5] *the variability of states of sea:* [6] *its* [2] *hydrostatic* [8] *quiescence in calm: its* [2] *hydrokinetic* [8] *turgidity in neap and spring tides:* [2] *its subsidence after devastation:* [5] *its sterility in the circumpolar icecaps, arctic and antarctic:* [4] *its climatic and commercial significance:* [8] *its preponderance of 3 to 1 over the dry land of the globe:* [2] *its indisputable hegemony* [5] *extending in square leagues* [7] *over all the region below the subequatorial tropic of Capricorn:* [5] *the multisecular stability of its primeval basin: its luteofulvous bed:* [8] *its capacity to* [2] *dissolve and* [4] *hold in solution all soluble substances including millions of tons of the most precious metals: its slow erosions of peninsulas [and islands, its persistent formation of* [2] *homothetic islands, peninsulas* [5] *]* and downwardtending promontories:* [2] *its alluvial deposits:* [5] *its weight and volume and density:* [2] *its imperturbability in lagoons, [atolls]* and highland tarns:* [4] *its* [2] *gradation of colours in the torrid and* [4] *temperate and frigid zones: its vehicular ramifications in continental lakecontained streams and* [2] *confluent* [3] *oceanflowing rivers* [2] *with their tributaries* [3] *and transoceanic currents:* [2] *gulfstream, north and south equatorial courses:* [8] *its violence in seaquakes, waterspouts,* [2] *artesian wells, eruptions,* [4] *torrents,* [5] *eddies, freshets,* [4] *spates,* [5] *groundswells,* [7] *, watersheds, waterpartings, geysers, cataracts, whirlpools, maelstroms, inundations, deluges, cloudbursts:* [4] *its vast circumterrestrial ahorizontal curve:* [2] its secrecy in springs, *and latent humidity, revealed by rhabdomantic or hygrometric instruments and* [8] exemplified [by the well]** by the hole in the wall at Ashtown gate, *saturation of air, distillation of dew:* [8] *the simplicity of its composition, two* [1] *constituent* [4] *parts of hydrogen with one* [1] *constituent part* [4] *of oxygen:* [1] its healing virtues: *its buoyancy in the waters of the Dead Sea:* [1] *its persevering penetrativeness in runnels, gullies, inadequate dams, leaks on shipboard:* [4] its properties for cleansing, quenching thirst and fire, nourishing ~~plant life~~ *vegetation:* [4] *its infallibility as paradigm and paragon: its metamorphoses as vapour, mist, cloud,*

---

*These bracketed words, present in second typescript but not in first galley proof, were almost certainly accidentally omitted by the compositor of the first proof.

**These three words, present in the manuscript, were omitted by the typist of the first typescript.

rain, sleet, snow, hail:[8] its strength in rigid hydrants: *its variety of forms in loughs and bays and gulfs and bights and guts and lagoons and atolls and archipelagos and sounds and fjords and minches and*[5] *tidal*[8] *estuaries and arms of sea: its solidity in glaciers, icebergs, ice-floes:*[5] its docility in working *hydraulic*[1] millwheels, *turbines, dynamos,*[5] electric power stations, bleachworks, tanneries, scutchmills: its utility in canals, rivers, if navigable, *floating and graving docks:*[5] *its potentiality derivable from harnessed tides*[4] *or watercourses falling from level to level:*[5] *its submarine*[1] fauna and flora (*anacoustic, photophobe*)[8] *numerically,* [1] *if not literally,*[4] *the inhabitants of the globe: its ubiquity as constituting 90% of the human body:*[1] ~~its~~ *the*[4] noxiousness *of its effluvia*[4] in *lacustrine*[4] marshes, pestilential fens, faded ~~flowers~~ *flowerwater,*[8] stagnant pools in the waning moon.

A perfect nutshell (or waterdrop) example of Joyce's accretive method may be seen near the end of this passage, where an original four words are quadrupled to a final sixteen. After initially setting down "its fauna and flora" in the basic manuscript, Joyce spotted among his notes the two entries "submarine" and "fishes (numerically) inhabit earth," and so added seven words to produce "its submarine fauna and flora numerically the inhabitants of the globe." In the first typescript, prompted by his note "literally, numerically," he seized the opportunity for the sort of wordplay that abounds in the episode and placed "if not literally" after "numerically." The second typescript and two galley proofs passed without change, but the final page proof received a typically scientific Ithacan parenthesis with "(anacoustic, photophobe)."

Incredible as it seems, Joyce, in compiling this catalogue, by no means entirely drained the reservoir of his notesheets. There, floating among the sixty-two notes that were used for this question (an average of one note for approximately every eight words), are such unused terms as *Kylls, landings, roads, breakwater, coral reef, annual rainfall,* and *evaporation.* And as if all this were not enough, Joyce at one time apparently planned to construct a "land" catalogue to balance the water question, for mixed in with his water notes are unused entries like *plain, valley, steppes, plateau, desert, savannahs, pampas,* and *prairie.* But whatever curiosity we may have about the possible use of such material is considerably restrained by a sense of relief that it was, after all, not used. Even Joyce, lover of lists, sensed for once that enough is enough.

Errata

The textual evolution of so complex a work as *Ulysses* inevitably invites errors, and Ithaca had its full share. These errata fall into two large divisions, those of composition and those of publication, and each splits into two subdivisions. The errors of composition, committed by Joyce himself, involve inconsistencies or mistakes in the episode's content, and subdivide into those which escaped detection to survive in the final text and those which Joyce caught and killed before publication. The errors of publication, committed by typist or printer, involve injuries to the episode's typography (and often, as a result, to the content as well), and subdivide into accidental omissions, unnoticed by Joyce, of words or phrases before publication, and misprints ranging from extra commas to dropped lines at the time of publication or in later editions.

Predictably, errors committed by Joyce in composition which survived into the final text are relatively few — about half a dozen, all of very minor significance. Most of them, indeed, involving mistakes in mathematics, go unnoticed even by an alert reader. There is no need to dwell on them here; they will be pointed out later in a section devoted to a running commentary on the episode ("An Ithacan Glossary"). If Joyce, however, in piecing together the intricate fabric of Ithaca, failed to align perfectly every seam and edge, the wonder is not that he allowed a few mistakes to escape his careful attention, but that he managed to avoid making many more than he actually did. When one considers his eyesight, particularly weak during the fall and winter of 1921 when he was struggling to put Ithaca into final shape, the pressure of time as *Ulysses* subscribers complained about delay in publication, and the fact that Ithaca is the most objectively detailed and itemized of all the episodes (five buttons on that waistcoat, 14 C P in that gasflame), demanding special care in composition and infested with traps of inconsistency or contradiction, the scarcity of error in the final version is little short of miraculous.

Errors caught and corrected

Error is not, however, scarce in the earlier versions. The hair-breadth escapes Joyce underwent in detecting, at the last moment, glaring mistakes which had somehow maintained perversely charmed life through several drafts emphasize further the nearly perfect state of the published text (in content, that is, not typography). As a reader moves through the successive stages of manuscript, typescripts and proofs, these errors become oddly fascinating points of interest. One learns to watch for them, and breathing becomes a little tighter as one turns, say, in a second galley proof to a passage that has remained flawed throughout the manuscript, two typescripts and the first proof. Will Joyce see it this time? No matter that familiarity with the final text assures us that Everything Comes Out All Right in the End — the little drama still exists. The criminal may be safely jailed, but we like to know how and when he was apprehended.

Some of these fugitives from artistic justice are merely petty felons, with comparatively short careers. For example, in the first typescript Joyce adds a ninth solution to the problem of "What to do with our wives," but in the following question fails to make the necessary change in the phrase "the lastmentioned (eighth) solution" (686). It is not until the second galley proof, three drafts later that "(eighth)" is corrected to "(ninth)." Sometimes such minor errors persist up to the final page proof. Two of these concern Bloom's budget for the day (711), added to the first typescript. One is the omission from the budget of Bloom's donation of five shillings in memory of Patrick Dignam, and the other is, conversely, the inclusion of the item, "Loan (Stephen Dedalus) refunded−1. 7. 0," when Joyce has not yet written anything about Bloom making this refund. Both are rectified in the last proof: the Dignam donation is inserted, and a new question added earlier in the episode which repays Stephen's loan.

Still other mistakes appear at the very beginning, in the manuscript, and are not caught until the very end, as many as six drafts later. Bloom's height and the cost of his soap are two minor examples. In manuscript as Bloom falls into the front area he is "five feet nine inches and a half" tall, but in his missing-person advertisement he is "5 ft. 8½ inches," and the price of his soap, given as fourpence in The Lotos Eaters episode, is listed here as threepence. Both contradictions survive through manuscript revision, two typescripts and two galley proofs, and are corrected only in the final page proof.[11]

Some other lapses are not so trivial. In the manuscript there is no section of some half-dozen questions, present in the final text, in which Bloom sees and reflects on the two torn betting-tickets on his kitchen dresser. Instead, listed among the other contents of the dresser shelves is "a red betting ticket." The lengthy addition dealing with the torn tickets and Bloom's thoughts appears in the first typescript, but that "red betting ticket" is not removed from the dresser shelf. There it stays unnoticed through four drafts until the final proof, when Joyce, like Bloom with the *Freeman,* throws it away.

Occasionally Joyce pulls a boner so glaring that one wonders how anyone, let alone so painstaking a craftsman, could commit it in the first place. In the manuscript Bloom burns in the candleflame not the Agendath Netaim prospectus, but Martha Clifford's typed letter. Yet a few pages later Bloom deposits Martha's letter with its predecessors in his table drawer. And so matters stand through typescript and two galley proofs. Not until the final page proof does the Agendath prospectus replace the letter in "total combustion."[12]

These errors of composition, of course, did no harm. Joyce committed them and he corrected them. But the mistakes made in preparing Ithaca for publication, mistakes Joyce did not commit, are an entirely different matter.

Omissions by typist or printer

Close comparison of manuscript, typescript and proofs reveals that many words and phrases Joyce wrote for the episode were omitted through oversight of either typist or printer. Material present in one draft is mysteriously absent in the next. Some fifty words have been lost in this way.

When a word disappears like this between two immediately successive drafts, such as manuscript and first typescript, there can be no question about its fate: it has suffered an accidental death through carelessness. Of course there is always the possibility, in any given case, that Joyce later spotted the omission but decided against restitution. When Robert McAlmon typed some of the Penelope episode for Joyce, he inadvertently shifted some of Molly's thoughts out of their Joycean order, but even though the author noticed the changes he let them stand.[13] It is highly unlikely, however, that Joyce would fail to restore words that were not merely shifted, but completely omitted—if he once detected their loss. But his poor eyesight, the haste with which he was working, and the fact that most of the omissions do not violently disrupt the coherence of the text are all strong arguments that he simply did not notice the errors.

Some of these omissions are of minor importance. The italicized words in the following quotations are all present in manuscript, but do not appear in first typescript or, consequently, the book:

...the offering of three prizes of 10/-, 5/-, and 2/6 respectively *for competition* by the Shamrock, a weekly newspaper? (678)

In sloping, upright and backhands: Queen's Hotel, Queen's Hotel, *Queen's Hotel,* Queen's Ho... (684)

...their *vast* archeological...literatures... (688)

...an orchard, kitchen garden and vinery, *all* protected against illegal trespassers... (714)

...the prospectus claimed *notable* advantages... (722)

Other omissions are more serious. The book lists among the contents of Bloom's table drawer "a cameo brooch, property of Ellen Bloom (born Higgins), deceased" (721). Immediately following this in the manuscript, however, but absent from first typescript and book, is "a cameo scarfpin, property of Rudolph Bloom (born Virag), deceased." It is easy to see how the typist could overlook the second of two such homeographic phrases, but the balance of Joyce's description and the emphasis on Bloom's loneliness are thereby decreased.

Another omission concerns Bloom's thoughts about possible revenge on Molly and Blazes Boylan. The question in the book begins:

What retribution, if any?

> Assassination, never, as two wrongs did not make one right. Duel by combat, no. Divorce, not now. Exposure by mechanical artifice (automatic bed) or individual testimony (concealed ocular witness), not yet. Suit for damages by legal influence or simulation of assault with evidence of injuries sustained (self-inflicted), not impossibly. (733)

And the answer continues with other more positive and rational schemes. But Joyce intended Bloom to have still another wild idea. In manuscript and first typescript, after "not impossibly" above, is this phrase: "Hushmoney by moral influence, possibly." It balances the preceding thought perfectly, not only in diction but in its pecuniary nature. Because of an imperceptive typist, however, Bloom's possible hushmoney does not appear in the second typescript.

Blame for some losses falls on printer instead of typist. One of these must not only be attributed partly to Joyce himself, but may ultimately have received his sanction. After Bloom, lying beside Molly, ponders the retributive schemes quoted above, his feelings culminate in "Satisfaction at the ubiquity...of adipose female hemispheres..." (734). In an addition to the manuscript, Joyce changes this to "adipose anterior and posterior female hemispheres," and left it that way through two typescripts. Doubt set in at the first galley proof, where Joyce, for reasons perhaps best left unprobed, crossed out *anterior and.* Then he changed his mind once again and wrote "*laissez*" in the margin—to no avail, for the printer ignored the marginal counterorder and removed *anterior and* from the second proof. Since Joyce obviously had considered this phrase with some care, he most likely noticed the omission here, but decided to leave well enough alone. The hemispheres remained posterior only.

When writing is as highly charged with multiple significance as Joyce's is, the loss of a single word can sometimes seriously deplete the text. One of the most important and regrettable omissions concerns a central theme of the book. As Bloom stands with Stephen beneath Molly's lighted window, Joyce writes, "How did he elucidate the mystery of an invisible person, his wife Marion (Molly) Bloom...?" (702). In the second galley proof, Joyce added the word "attractive" before "person," but the printer failed to embody the addition in the page proof. As a result a key word describing the relationship between Molly and Bloom, and, far more important, suggesting the effect of Molly on Stephen, is lost.

At other times we cannot be certain that omissions are accidental. These are cases where Joyce may have cancelled words, but we cannot be sure. His habit, for example, of deleting words not by crossing them out but by enclosing them in parentheses probably cheated the final text more than once. Most of these places are clear enough: when the manuscript reads, "an empty (jar of) pot of Plumtree's potted meat," the typist can ignore the parenthesis with a clear conscience. But Ithaca is full of intentional parentheses, and they must have caused trouble. At one point, indeed, where some enclosures appeared improbable — "to whom (which)...which it (he)" (694) — Joyce foresaw the danger and instructed the typist in the margin, "*écrivez les paroles en parentheses.*" But the following parentheses, all omitted from the typescript, are probably innocent victims:

"a battery of jamjars (empty) of various sizes" (675)

"sent to Miss Marion (Molly) Tweedy" (678)

"Mrs Riordan (Dante), a widow" (680)

"The marquess of Ripon and (honest) John Morley" (717)

"addressed (erroneously) to Mrs L. Bloom with brief accompanying note commencing (erroneously): Dear Madam" (721)

Other occasions where we cannot be sure whether a phrase was cancelled by Joyce or dropped accidentally arise when some portion of the typescript is missing. A lost page of first typescript, for example, can prevent us from determining the fate of words which are present in manuscript but fail to appear in the second typescript. The extreme rarity of Joycean deletion, however, makes these omissions suspect. Here is one almost certainly accidental:

The indoor exercises...were to be made with mental concentration in front of a mirror so as to bring into play the various families of muscles and produce successively a *pleasant rigidity, a more* pleasant relaxation and the most pleasant repristination of juvenile agility. (681)

The italicized words appear in the manuscript but are absent from the first galley proof. The typescript for this passage is missing, but it is hard to believe that Joyce cancelled these four words. For one thing, "*pleasant*" and "*more pleasant*" complete the comparative progression ending in the text's "most pleasant." Moreover, an entry in the British Museum note-sheets reads, "Mind develops muscle exercise before glass stiffness pleasanter." The final text uses everything in this note except "stiffness," which is supplied by the missing "rigidity." Finally, comparison of manuscript and proof reveals that, except for this single omission, no other change whatever was made in the missing typescript page. With this evidence, we must arraign either the typist or the printer of the first proof.

A very similar case appears in the following passage: "...socalled fixed stars, in reality evermoving *wanderers* from immeasurably remote eons to infinitely remote futures..." (698) The word *wanderers* appears in manuscript, first and second typescript, but not in first galley proof. It is barely possible that Joyce deleted it in a missing third typescript, but if he did, again it was the only change he made—and we have no definite evidence that Joyce ever revised the third typescript at any time. Once again, too, a rough note indicates that the missing word belongs in the passage: "During vast, starspeckled night. Wanderers of the ages. Restless." There can be little doubt that carelessness is responsible for loss of the word which neatly prepares for the later "Ever he would wander...beyond the fixed stars..." (727).

Omission of the following nine italicized words from the "water hymn" is also probably accidental: "its slow erosions of peninsulas *and islands, its persistent formation of homothetic islands, peninsulas* and downwardtending promontories" (672). The missing words are present in the second typescript, but not in galley proof. Again, as with *wanderers* above, Joyce may have deleted this passage in a missing third typescript, but it is highly unlikely. Since the text is interrupted at the word "peninsulas," and the lost passage ends with that same word, the eyes of the copyist most probably skipped from the first "peninsulas" to the second, giving Ithaca an unkind cut in the process.

Other cases are not so clearly weighted on one side. When Bloom and Stephen are discussing Hebrew and Gaelic, the text asks, "How was a glyphic comparison of the phonic symbols of both languages made in substantiation of the oral comparison?" (688) The opening words of the answer, in manuscript, are "By juxtaposition." The first typescript here is missing, and these two words themselves are missing in the second typescript. Joyce or typist? The words are a marginal addition to the manuscript, and so might more easily be overlooked by the typist, but conclusions cannot be drawn from evidence like this.

Molly misplaced several volumes in Bloom's library. It is possible that typist or printer has completely lost one. In the catalogue of Bloom's books, immediately after *"The Child's Guide* (blue cloth)" (708) manuscript and first typescript list *"The Beauties of Killarney* (wrappers)." The second typescript is missing, and there is no sign of the title in the first galley proof. It would be easy, of course, to skip a line in copying this list, and almost as easy for Joyce to overlook the omission. Moreover, intentional deletion is unlikely, for Killarney has significance as a minor theme throughout *Ulysses*: Bloom wants to see a performance of *The Lily of Killarney* (92, 380) and dreams of visiting the lakes of Killarney (726); Stephen sees a *Pocket Guide to Killarney* on a bookstall (242). There are other references, and Killarney becomes one of many motifs associated with travel, the promised land, and Molly-substitutes. This is of course no proof that Joyce did not delete the title, but it does suggest that something more has been removed than merely a clever listing which places wrappers around ambiguous beauties.

Misprints

"I am extremely irritated by all those printer's errors," Joyce complained while reading proofs. "Are these to be perpetuated in future editions? I hope not."[14] And after *Ulysses* was published he spoke particularly of Ithaca: "Some of the blunders and omissions which disfigure *Ithaca* especially are lamentable."[15] Unfortunately, not only were many of the errors perpetuated in later editions, but new errors were perpetrated through the corruptions of pirated texts.

It is now well known that the first authorized American edition of *Ulysses* (New York: Random House–Modern Library, 1934) was set up from the text of a pirated edition printed for the unscrupulous Samuel Roth. The Random House edition thus inherited the large number of errors from the earlier unauthorized printing, and added a few more of its own for good measure. Many of these were corrected in later printings, especially in the reset edition of 1961, but the text is still badly flawed. It is the purpose of the present section to establish an accurate text for Ithaca.

Since the French printers of *Ulysses* were working with a foreign language, Joyce had more than the usual trouble all authors experience in proofreading. He corrected *carers* to *careers,* only to have it come back *carreers.* He straightened out the garbled word order in a passage by drawing an arrow to the proper position, and when the next proof simply scrambled the passage even further, he patiently numbered in proper sequence each of the nine words involved. Despite his irritation at "those printer's errors," however, Joyce must share the responsibility for the survival of many of them: working hastily with poor vision, he missed many errors in his proofreading. The best example of this is the misprint "reserved" in the description of the cryptogram in Bloom's table drawer (721). Although Joyce's manuscript read "reversed," the typist copied it as "reserved," and it stayed that way right into publication. Joyce failed to notice the error even though he twice returned to this same sentence in proof to make other revisions.[16] Occasionally, in fact, Joyce himself committed mistakes which his printer faithfully copied. In a page proof he "corrected" *Tiperary* to *Tiperrary,* and in another place one of his big words (and his little Greek) tripped him: he added the word *boustrophedontic,* but misspelled it *boustrephodontic* (the second *t* is also usually omitted). Both of these went into print and were corrected only in later editions.

Sometimes Joyce's difficulties culminated in comic irony. He took special pains with that large dot which serves as answer to the last question of the episode, "Where?" In his manuscript margin he explained to the typist, "*La réponse à la dernière demande est un point,*" but he forgot to give the same warning to the printer, and the dot failed to appear in galley proof. Joyce marked it in and scrawled, *"Comme réponse un point bien visible."* When the final page proof came through with nothing but an ordinary period, he insisted, *"Le point doit être plus visible,"* and the published book displayed a quite satisfactory dot. The battle was won—until the Modern Library edition sabotaged all by neglecting to get the point.

The following lists of errors in the Ithaca text are the result of close study of all prepublication materials—notes, manuscript, typescript and proofs—and collation with the first Shakespeare and Company edition (February 1922), the eighth printing of this edition (1926), when the text was entirely reset with many corrections, the Odyssey Press edition (1932), which Stuart Gilbert supervised at Joyce's request, the first Modern Library edition (1934), and the reset Modern Library edition (1961). The three lists are identified by their headings, but the first in particular needs a word of explanation. Because of widespread sales, the 1934 Modern Library edition is still the only copy owned by many readers, and so its errors are listed here even though corrected in the 1961 edition. The second list, of 1934 errors repeated in 1961, is of course aimed at the owner of either edition, while the third list, of new errors in 1961, naturally concerns only the owners of that edition.

1. Errata in 1934 Modern Library edition, corrected in 1961 edition (page references to 1934).

658.2	close parenthesis after (*convected*
659.21	insert comma after *redolent*
662.21	Joyce's proof instruction about the typography of POLDY's acrostic verse could also apply to the 1934 Modern Library edition: *"Imprimez ces lettres initiales avec des types plus foncés."*
679.1	delete comma after *process*
684.26	for *statosphere* read *stratosphere*
686.6	for *suppositous* read *suppositious*
687.17	for *indefiinitely* read *indefinitely*
688.3	for *unnecessarily* read *unnecessary*
691.3	for *cicrumstantial* read *circumstantial*
694	in the paragraph beginning *"Short but yet..."* the letter "s," wherever it appears medially, should be printed in its antiquated form (resembling the letter "f"). Joyce twice instructed the printer on this, once in the typescript (*Note—dans ce paragraphe employez pour les "s" les vieux types "S"*) and again in proof (*si possible employez pour ces lettres les "s" ancienne en forme de "S"*).

694.27	for *volume or* read *volume of*
698.1	insert comma after *border*
700.17	for *Arrange* read *Arranged*
702.19	for *of odds* read *at odds*
702.24	delete comma after *blue*
704.6	insert comma after (*Laird line*)
705.10	for *wander* read *wonder*
706.24	delete comma after *biceps 9 in.*
708.15	close parenthesis after (*respectively*
708.33	for *sucide* read *suicide*
709.3	delete comma after *hebdomadary*
718.10	for *condition* read *conditions*

2. Errata in both 1934 and 1961 Modern Library editions (first page reference 1934, second 1961). Starred items are accidental prepublication omissions, as distinguished from typographical misprints or errors intruding after publication.

650.1/666.1	for *courses* read *course*
653.2/669.1–2	although *indication* should be *indiction* and *MXMIV* should be *MCMIV,* Joyce himself wrote the erroneous form in each case.
*656.2/672.3	after *peninsulas* insert *and islands, its persistent formation of homothetic islands, peninsulas*
*656.4/672.5	after *lagoons* insert comma and *atolls*
*656.15/672.16	after *exemplified* insert *by the well*
659.19/675.19	insert comma after *one*
*662.1/678.1	after *respectively* insert *for competition*
*665.31/681.28	after *successively* insert *pleasant rigidity, a more*
*668.35/684.31	insert a third repetition of *Queen's hotel* preceded and followed by a comma
672.19/688.11	for *entitled* read *entituled*
*673.1/688.30	before *archeological* insert *vast*
679.17/694.37	for *not for her she expressed* read *to her she expressed*
*683.20/698.34	after *evermoving* insert *wanderers*
684.37/700.13	for *and all* read *and to all*
*687.8/702.24	after *invisible* insert *attractive*
691.14/706.29	delete comma after *sustained*
692.32/708.9	for *creator* read *procreator*
697.29/712.38	for *then 5* read *than 15*
*698.39/714.7	before *protected* insert *all*
702.25/717.36	insert comma after *paper*
704.12/719.23	after *Holland and* insert *for Liverpool Underwriters'*

	Association, the cost of acquired rolling stock (these ten words, present in proofs and first edition, disappeared when the text was reset for the eighth printing in 1926)
704.37/720.8	after *20 years* insert *are*
*705.39/721.11	after *deceased:* insert *a cameo scarfpin, property of Rudolph Bloom (born Virag), deceased:*
706.3/721.14	for *reserved* read *reversed*; the second "t" in *boustrophedontic* is Joyce's — the OED lists only *boustrophedonic*; *punctated* is not a misprint
*706.32/722.2	before *advantages* insert *notable*
710.31/726.4	for *nothing or* read *nothing, nothing or*
711.8/726.17	for *now* read *not*
713.28/728.38	for *Thummin* read *Thummim*
715.38/731.8	for *adder* read *adders*
716.37/732.8	insert comma after *transmitted*
*718.27/733.37	after *impossibly.* insert *Hushmoney by moral influence, possibly.*
722/737	in answer to the last question, a large black dot (Corrected in Modern Library paperback edition)

3. New errata in 1961 Modern Library edition

675.19	insert comma after *one*
678.38	insert comma after *Bouverist*
681.23	*Eugen Sandow's* first name here is not a misprint; later, in the catalogue of Bloom's books, Joyce misspelled it *Eugene*
681.33	for *table* read *stable*
684.12	for *is* read *in*
687.22	for *Neubkim* read *Nebukim*
731.35	for *nolast* read *no last*
732.23	insert comma after *nature*
734.4	for *void incertitude* read *void of incertitude*
734.8	*self abbreviating* should be one word
737.24	delete *a* before *dark*

Part Two

A Critical Study of Ithaca

4

"This Frightful Text"

In the fall of 1921, when Joyce completed the fair copy of Ithaca and announced that *Ulysses* was finished, he wistfully remarked to Robert McAlmon, "*Ithaca* is very strange. I wonder will you like it."[1]

All critics agree it is very strange, and for many years most of them did not like it. The reaction of William Empson, no stranger to difficult texts, may perhaps best summarize the critical consensus. During a BBC talk in which he struggled to get at the meaning of *Ulysses* in the Ithaca episode, Empson suddenly paused, and although he had already spoken of "the appalling style of this chapter," interjected in almost comic desperation, "You understand I am trying to interpret this frightful text."[2]

Empson had distinguished company. Edmund Wilson spoke of the question-and-answer technique as "the most opaque and uninviting medium possible," and lumping Ithaca together with Oxen of the Sun and Eumaeus, called the triad "colorless and tiresome," "a dead weight," and with pontific finality, "artistically absolutely indefensible."[3] The word "painful" became a favorite. To Harry Levin the Ithacan dialectic was "unrelievedly painful and banal,"[4] and to David Daiches "painfully objective";[5] even in later criticism Richard Ellmann could speak of "this painfully rational chapter."[6] Philip Toynbee simply refused to discuss the episode: "I shall say nothing of the seventy-page question-and-answer section...because it has become, and not unjustly, the *point de mire* of all hostile critics."[7] Joseph Prescott, on the other hand, was driven to scornful exclamation: "And the scene at Bloom's house...presented in the form of an examination paper! This sort of writing is chock-full of the boredom which poisons the pleasure of the reader in other parts of *Ulysses.*"[8]

Although there were notable exceptions to this chorus of disapproval (William York Tindall, or Hugh Kenner, for example), Joycean criticism in the three or four decades after the novel's publication quickly established an adverse majority opinion about Ithaca. All this greatly changed in the next twenty or so years, when the significance and merit of the episode became increasingly recognized in a series of detailed studies by such better-stationed critics as S. L. Goldberg, Stanley Sultan, Marilyn French, C. H. Peake, Suzette Henke, and others. This does not mean that anyone finds Ithaca easy going; all attest to its difficulty. A. Walton Litz writes, "Any reading of *Ulysses* that aims at doing justice to Joyce's complex vision must be composed of constant adjustments and accommodations between myth and fact, and it is in 'Ithaca' that these adjustments are most difficult to make." [9] And Marilyn French rightly surmises that a reader can easily believe Ithaca to be "one great piece of nonsense," appearing as "a series of irrelevant parallels, contrasts, quantitative relations, and inter-meshings of totally inane crossing points." [10] But it is also Marilyn French who reflects a revised consensus when she proposes that Ithaca is "probably the greatest chapter in the novel." [11]

"Frightful," "indefensible," "chock-full of boredom": Ithaca is nothing of the kind. Judgments like these, suspect in their extremity, uncloak misunderstanding; they clearly reveal that whatever merits Ithaca may possess, it also possesses strong barriers to understanding and appreciation. Only when these barriers, these causes of critical consternation, are identified can one see the real Ithaca that lives behind them.

The difficulty of Ithaca, as in so much of Joyce, lies less in what is said than in how it is said. Technique, not content, is the major trouble-maker. [12] The reader who enters Ithaca for the first time is immediately struck and, as just noted, often repelled by four closely related features of Joyce's technique, and the first of these is the question-and-answer method itself. Even brother Stanislaus was perplexed: "I don't understand the intention of the catechism." [13]

"I have a book at home" Stephen tells Lynch during their discussion of aesthetics in *A Portrait of the Artist,* "in which I have written down questions which are more amusing than yours were. In finding the answers to them I found the theory of the esthetic which I am trying to explain. Here are some of the questions I set myself: *Is a chair finely made tragic or comic? Is the portrait of Mona Lisa good if I desire to see it? Is the bust of Sir Philip Crampton lyrical, epical or dramatic? If not, why not? If a man hacking in fury at a block of wood . . . make there an image of a cow, is that image a work of art? If not, why not?"* (214, corrected text, New York: The Viking Press, 1964).

Stephen's creator did have such a book. In 1903, while in Paris on his test flight from Dublin, Joyce kept a notebook for random philosophical and artistic observations. Working out his aesthetic theories, he set himself questions like the following to test his definition that "Art is the human disposition of sensible or intelligible matter for an aesthetic end":

Question:	*Why are not excrements, children and lice works of art?*
Answer:	Excrements, children and lice are human products — human dispositions of sensible matter. The process by which they are produced is natural and non-artistic; their end is not an aesthetic end: therefore they are not works of art.
Question:	*Can a photograph be a work of art?*
Answer:	A photograph is a disposition of sensible matter and may be so disposed for an aesthetic end but it is not a human disposition of sensible matter. Therefore it is not a work of art.
Question:	*If a man hacking in fury at a block of wood make there an image of a cow (say) has he made a work of art?*
Answer:	The image of a cow made by a man hacking in fury at a block of wood is a human disposition of sensible matter but it is not a human disposition of sensible matter for an aesthetic end. Therefore it is not a work of art.
Question:	*Are houses, clothes, furniture, etc., works of art?*
Answer:	Houses, clothes, furniture, etc., are not necessarily works of art. They are human dispositions of sensible matter. When they are so disposed for an aesthetic end they are works of art.[14]

Thus among Joyce's earliest prose are the incunabula of the interrogative method later used as background in the Nestor episode, foreground in Ithaca, and, it might be said, as back-, fore-, and underground in the classroom-quiz and inquisition-of-Yawn sections of *Finnegans Wake* (Part I, Ch. 6, and Part III, Ch. 3). It is a method evolving ultimately from the fundamental curiosity of inquisitive man in an incomprehensible universe, for what is Ithaca but the inevitable development of the first tentative, prehistoric "Why?" which cursed — and glorified — the consciousness of rational man? Of the many historical precedents for Ithaca, including Socratic dialogue, legal inquiry, pedagogical examination, scientific method, and even modern advertising ("What is home without Plumtree's Potted Meat?"), two at least exerted special influence — religious catechism and scholastic dialectic: Jesuit-trained Joyce, "Steeled in the school of old Aquinas" ("The Holy Office"), sharpened his intellectual teeth on question and answer, problem and solution, theory and demonstration. In asking and answering the questions of the episode which is his *Summa* of Bloom and Everyman, he must have felt, as did Stephen about his aesthetic, that St. Thomas "will carry me all along the line." In method, Ithaca is "applied Aquinas" (*A Portrait*, 209).[15]

The interrogative method, then is the first and most apparent of the four barriers confronting the reader. In itself, however, it should not be particularly strange or difficult to accept: no one has ever accused the

Socratic dialogues of being "artistically absolutely indefensible." Not the interrogation itself, but the way it is carried out makes Ithaca's questions and answers so disturbing, and this manner evolves automatically—all too automatically—from the other three barriers. Hugh Kenner names all three: "The impersonality of the 'Ithaca' catechism is...an immense parody of pseudo-Flaubertian 'scientific' detachment."[16] Science, Flaubertian naturalism, and aesthetic detachment or indifference—these are Ithaca's immediate foundations. All three are vitally interdependent: science is the generator of literary naturalism, and disinterested detachment characterizes both.

Little needs to be said about science in Ithaca, where the reader revisits his college Chem I lab. The "Art" of the episode, in Joyce's schema for *Ulysses,* is science, and he himself called the section "a mathematico-astronomico-physico-mechanico-geometrico-chemico sublimation of Bloom and Stephen," where "all events are resolved into their cosmic, physical, psychical, etc. equivalents."[17] As already seen, Joyce went to deliberate extremes in his rough notes to soak himself in scientific data and jargon. As a result, even the most personal of human relationships, the sexual, is impersonalized into the mechanical "energetic piston and cylinder movement" (732). Or consider mathematics: two-thirds of the numbers listed in Hanley's *Word Index to James Joyce's Ulysses* are located in Ithaca, which forms less than a tenth of the novel. Actually, Ithaca's "science" is about as authentic as the electrical pyrotechnics in a Hollywood production of *Frankenstein,* but this is not immediately apparent to the initiate reader. For him, Ithaca's science makes difficult any serious consideration of the episode as "art," and the barrier is formidable.

Speaking of *Ulysses* as a whole, but certainly with Ithaca dominantly in mind, Wyndham Lewis complained of Joyce's "painful preoccupation with the *exact* place of things in a room, for instance," and announced, with a hint of critical hysteria, "It is the very nightmare of the naturalistic method."[18] He is right, but nightmare that it is, Ithaca is not without precedent in the naturalist tradition. In regarding a germinal work like *Madame Bovary,* for example, one is startled by passages which sound like direct models for Ithaca. The answers to the invented questions below are quotations from Flaubert's novel, but they could easily pass muster as excerpts from Joyce:

Describe Bovary's hat.

Oval, stiffened with whalebone, it began with three round bands; then came in succession lozenges of velvet and rabbit-skin separated by red bands; after that a sort of bag that ended in a cardboard polygon covered with complicated braiding, from which hung, at the end of a long thin cord, small twisted gold threads in the manner of a tassel.

What homothetic objects occupied Bovary's living-quarters?

Behind the door hung a cloak with a small collar, a bridle, and a black leather cap, and on the floor, in a corner, were a pair of leggings, still covered with dry mud.... A canary-yellow paper, relieved at the top by a garland of pale flowers, was puckered everywhere over the badly-stretched canvas; white calico curtains with a red border hung crossways the length of the window; and on the mantlepiece a clock with a head of Hippocrates shone resplendent between two silver-plated candlesticks under oval shades.... Volumes of the "Dictionary of Medical Science," uncut, but the binding rather the worse for the successive sales through which they had gone, occupied almost alone the six shelves of a deal bookcase.[19]

Vocabulary, phrasing, and detail in these passages are uncannily Ithacan. But Flaubert can go even further. In the harangues of Homais the druggist, circumlocutory, pedantic, and jargonistic, appear passages which fully equal even the most absurdly pompous moments of Ithaca. Here is one of the best:

The thermometer...falls in winter to 4 degrees, and in the hottest season rises to 25 or 30 degrees Centigrade at the outside, which gives us 24 degrees Réamur as the maximum, or otherwise 54 degrees Fahrenheit (English scale), not more...and this heat, moreover, which, on account of the aqueous vapors given off by the river and the considerable number of cattle in the fields, which...exhale much ammonia, that is to say, nitrogen, hydrogen, and oxygen (no, nitrogen and hydrogen alone), and which sucking up into itself the humus from the ground, mixing together all those different emanations...and combining with the electricity diffused through the atmosphere, when there is any, might in the long run, as in tropical countries, engender insalubrious miasmata....[20]

All this, however, is Flaubert at his naturalistic and satiric extreme; *Madame Bovary* as a whole is of course by no means so overwhelmingly particularistic or inflated. But Ithaca from beginning to end seems, to repeat Lewis' protest, to be a "nightmare of the naturalistic method," and the reader reacts accordingly. An unbearably absurd naturalism joins interrogation and science as a third barrier to the acceptance of Ithaca.

Both scientist and literary naturalist, almost by definition, must maintain or appear to maintain detachment. The world, in reality or fiction, is to be examined with icy objectivity, and nowhere in the entire canon of Joyce's work is his aesthetic theory of indifference carried further than in Ithaca. In defining the highest form of literature, Stephen, in *A Portrait,* says, "The artist, like the God of the creation, remains within or behind or above his handiwork, invisible, refined out of existence, indifferent, paring his nails" (215). Speaking of Joyce's "essential neutrality of...purpose and attitude," David Daiches says that "the painfully objective catechism of the 'Ithaca' episode is of all the styles the most faithful to Joyce's attitude as revealed by the scope and nature of *Ulysses.*"[21] Precisely, exclaims the reader — what neutrality! What objectivity! The Bloom we have come almost to love is now reduced to a pitiable creature paring *his* nails in the lonely solitude of his front room. An inhuman artist stares mercilessly at his human subjects, and the reader, infuriated at meeting this final barrier, turns away for good.

Interrogative method, science, naturalism, and indifference — these, then, are the four barriers to understanding and appreciation in Ithaca. Taken together, and it is impossible to separate them, they produce an attitude and style of ruthless analysis. Fiction written like this, it would seem, deserves to be condemned, and many readers, seeing little further than this, are unhesitating in their judgment. And as if this were not enough, Joyce doubles and trebles the effect by using every means of exaggeration and intensification at his disposal. The questions are outrageously tedious and maddeningly incessant; the terminology resembles an indiscriminate mash of "quashed quotatoes," to borrow a *Finnegans Wake* phrase, from scientific manuals; naturalistic details are amassed to such an extent that Wyndham Lewis deplored "the constipation induced in the movement of the narrative";[22] and indifference, it seems, is carried to a point of frigid insensibility. As a result, the reader who might have been willing, even if only for the sake of argument, as it were, to accept an objective technique is repelled by the apparently fantastic lengths to which Joyce has gone.

But the reader who stops at this point has not realized that all of this adds up to parody. To repeat Kenner's description with a different emphasis, "The impersonality of the 'Ithaca' catechism is...*an immense parody of pseudo*-Flaubertian 'scientific' detachment." Science, for example, is treated so thoroughly, so solemnly, that it collapses under its own weight. As Joyce here employs one of his favorite methods, inflation for the sake of deflation, science becomes simultaneously the *summum bonum* and *reductio ad absurdum* of modern man. And as with science, so does Ithaca embody the final extreme, the ultra-logical dead end, of naturalism. It, too, becomes its own executioner. Lewis' complaint about the nightmarish naturalism of *Ulysses* is simply unwitting testimony, at least so far as Ithaca is concerned, that Joyce has accomplished precisely his purpose. The naturalism of the episode even suggests a kind of parody, in reverse, of the *Odyssey*: there, the disguised Ulysses answers almost all questions with thumping lies, whereas Joyce's answers are the truth, the whole truth, and nothing but the truth, so help him Flaubert. Any understanding of

Ithaca, then, must begin with the recognition that its techniques are all accomplices in the ulterior purpose of parody. But this is still only the beginning. Sympathetic readers can get this far and still fail to detect, or appreciate fully, many important qualities in the episode.

The interrogative method, besides its strangeness as a narrative technique, can be troublesome in other ways. The problem of point of view bothers some readers. Through whose eyes, in this impersonal catechism, are we looking at Bloom and Stephen? Who is conducting the interrogation? The dramatis personae is somehow incomplete: there are Bloom, Stephen, and Molly, but where is the questioner? Where the answerer? This problem, clearly, is closely related to the barrier of the artist's detachment. The author here has tried to refine himself out of existence, yet someone must be asking those questions—someone very persistent and thorough indeed, someone very much "present." That someone, of course, detachment or indifference notwithstanding, is Joyce, and not merely in the obvious sense that he is the composer of the episode. He not only wrote the drama of Ithaca, he assigned himself a speaking part as well. There he is, gleam in eye and tongue in cheek, clearly enjoying his role as grand inquisitor. And he who asks is also answering. This is a one-man catechism, a double role, an apparently impossible dialectical soliloquy, and it is this tour de force which, needlessly, can disturb the undiscerning reader.

A related question can also be troublesome here: when, in the answers, does the omniscient author who is responding to his own questions couch his replies in the words or thoughts of Bloom, when in those of Stephen, and when in his own terms only? The great majority of answers present indirectly the voice or mind of Bloom; a few do the same for Stephen. But many are simply descriptive and must not be assumed to originate with either Bloom or Stephen. To imagine, for example, that the involved description of water flowing from reservoir to kitchen sink is taking place in Bloom's mind is as mistaken as the supposition, made by one reader, that "the action of the faucet is analyzed by the director of the water works."[23] But occasionally there can be confusion. One such passage occurs when the pair step outside "into the penumbra of the garden" (698). There they see "The heaventree of stars hung with humid nightblue fruit." Although the poetic imagery here is a clue, the reader does not learn until four pages later, when Bloom disagrees it is a heaventree (701), that this line is spoken aloud by Stephen. Immediately afterward come the twin macrocosm-microcosm answers, the first explicitly identified as Bloom's "demonstration to his companion of various constellations," but the second merely labeled "obverse meditations of involution increasingly less vast." Are these latter also Bloom's? At first they appear to belong to Stephen. Bloom, so far as we know, has no knowledge of such things as "the universe of human serum constellated with red and white bodies." The "involution" of the question is what we might expect from the introspective Stephen, and its conclusion, "if the progress were carried far enough, nought nowhere was never reached," is typical Dedalian cynicism. But in the next question—"Why did he not elaborate these calculations to a more precise result?"—the pronoun, with its reference to the "Bloom" of more than 300 words earlier, reveals that these "obverse meditations," like the original "meditations," are also Leopoldian. "Scientific" Bloom's smattering of knowledge is just enough to carry him along until he peters out into that "nought nowhere."

The question-and-answer technique can hinder the reader in another way, this time without his realizing it. Even after repeated readings, Ithaca's many questions may continue to be regarded as discrete units, or at best as a loosely assembled series of units. As a result, too many readers fail to perceive the episode's tight coherence of construction. Most of the questions are indeed worthy of separate contemplation; many, in fact, demand extremely close scrutiny before yielding full significance. But taken in sequence, they also constitute a remarkably coherent narrative line. For example, consider Bloom's movements and thoughts in his front room after Stephen has left. Everything is carefully accounted for or motivated; nothing is arbitrary or purposeless. As Bloom enters the room he strikes his head on the walnut sideboard, shifted by Molly during the day to a new position. The succeeding questions advance in close causal relationship from this point. Bloom elevates his candle to survey the rearranged scene, and the furniture is described. He sees and smells the stain on the large easychair and consequently lights a cone of incense, using the Agendath Netaim prospectus as a torch. When he burns this folder in the candledish on the mantle, he sees first the clock, owl and dwarf tree there, then his own image in the mirror behind them, and finally the reflection of his books, some of which are inverted. Straightening the books, he notes the two-volume *History of the Russo-Turkish War,* tries to remember the name of a battle, fails, takes a volume to the table (because the work is the "largest in bulk" in his library), sits down, and promptly remembers. There he is, then, ready for compiling budgets, building dream-houses, and fondling schemes for easy wealth. The narrative from bumped head to remembered battle consumes five pages and nineteen questions, yet nothing has been irrelevantly introduced. Each question, born of its predecessor, generates its successor.

It is not the interrogative method, however, that causes most of the difficulty in understanding and appreciating Ithaca. The major stumbling block is the author's attitude of cold, super-scientific indifference. David Daiches, as noted earlier, selected Ithaca as the best example of Joyce's "essential neutrality of...purpose and attitude." But Daiches does not stop with this. After discussing Joyce's purpose of indifference and singling out Ithaca as its extreme demonstration, he launches a determined attack on that purpose: "There are some—and their number is growing—who are beginning to realize anew the truth, forgotten by a generation, that the indifference of the artist is a snare and a delusion, an impossibility, a ridiculous abstraction, a lie exposed by the very fact that the writer puts pen to paper at all. If the artist were really indifferent he would not write.... Of course Joyce was deceiving himself, and that is why that complete, flat, static craftsman's world of his is not our world at all, nor anybody's world, but an artist's misunderstanding."[24] And he adds finally that such indifference is the resort of a sensitive artist who is afraid to implicate himself in our chaotic modern world, and who thus becomes a measure of the decay of twentieth-century civilization.

It is not artist but critic who is guilty of misunderstanding here. Daiches mistakenly equates aesthetic indifference with what might be called functional or operative indifference. He assumes that if an artist endorses indifference as an aesthetic theory or literary technique, he also extends that indifference to his actual relations with the world about him, and hence, logically, should even abstain from creative activity. Of course aesthetic indifference is an illusion, but it is a deliberate and conscious illusion, not "a delusion...a lie." Every page of *Ulysses* testifies vividly that Joyce was anything but indifferent to his world, and his decision to keep himself out of his work does nothing to alter that fact.

The Ithaca episode, where indifference appears to be carried almost to the point of inhumanity, is particularly vulnerable to a critical misunderstanding of this sort. After all, Joyce himself said, "...the reader will know everything and know it in the baldest and coldest way."[25] As far as they go, critics who emphasize Ithaca's coldness, whether approvingly or not, are of course right—but often they do not go far enough. Many fail to see that the episode, not only in spite of its objectivity, but often precisely because of it, contains much that is warm, subjective, and movingly human.

The most obvious human quality intensified by the inhuman objectivity in Ithaca is humor. Yet too many readers have failed to appreciate the full scope of the episode's comedy, and reactions range all the way from Joseph Prescott's "chock-full of boredom" to the votes of Tindall and Kenner for Ithaca as the funniest section in *Ulysses*.[26] Much of this humor resides precisely in what would seem to preclude it—the elaborate conglomeration of jargon, circumlocution, detail, parallelism and antithesis, dedicated to all that is solemn, logical, exact and complete. "This frightful text" rings with the laughter of the absurd, the cumulative, the overdone, the extreme, and the tone of cold detachment intensifies all: deliberate humorlessness is the source of much of Ithaca's fun. With no hint of the barest smile, ludicrous events or subjects are discussed in earnest, dead-pan gravity. Instead of being told, for example, that Bloom sits motionless and silent simply because he is tired, we are told that his passivity is "In accordance with the law of the conservation of energy" (692). Frank Budgen writes, "The same toneless, unhuman voice invites us to contemplate tragic and comic happenings and happenings of no importance. The comic of *Ithaca* is the terrible comic of masks, the comic of the comedian who always keeps a straight face."[27] And even Daiches, who attacked artistic indifference as "a ridiculous abstraction," grants that Joyce's "supreme aloofness...makes supreme comedy."[28]

Joyce's aloofness, combined with his super-scientific, ultra-naturalistic parody, is comic in still another, more literally organic way. The tone of Ithaca is intended to continue the stylistic portrayal of the effects of drunkenness which began in the Oxen of the Sun episode, culminated in Circe, and became after-effects in Eumaeus. Readers are quickly aware that the wild and whirling words of the last pages of Oxen of the Sun and most of Circe present the state of advanced intoxication in which Stephen, particularly, and Bloom, in his fashion, find themselves. And it is not hard to recognize, in the exhausted language of Eumaeus, the beginning of the sobering-up process. Joyce, with plenty of personal experience to draw upon, knew that the bacchanalian frenzy of such a *Walpurgisnacht* as Stephen experiences in Bella Cohen's parlor is immediately followed by two distinct, if imperceptibly merging, states of mind and feeling. The first, seen in Eumaeus, is an emotional and mental collapse into lethargy. Nothing matters. Torpor dominates the system. This state gradually gives way to a second, where apathy is replaced by an abnormal clarity and focus. The convalescent views all about him — and himself as well — with a sense of utter detachment and objectivity. He seems to be apart from, and slightly above, his surroundings, and regards even his own actions with an indifferent curiosity as though he were looking at someone else. Still nothing really matters, but how clinically interesting everything is. How keenly sharp, how factually precise, how fully susceptible to impartial analysis everything has become. Here is the style of Ithaca in all its mock sobriety.[29]

Budgen has also said, "Joyce's sense of humor was of a tonic and refreshing kind that delighted in strange words, puns, incongruities, odd situations, exaggerations and impish angles of vision."[30] He is speaking here of *Ulysses* as a whole, but every term in his list applies eminently to Ithaca. Joyce's revisions and additions during composition, examined in Part One, revealed constant and subtle play on words, particularly through

etymology. Here is the linguist, to give still another example, who apprehended and imprisoned in his notesheets the fine word "thaumaturgic,"
hoping to find a suitable place for it. In the second typescript he saw the
perfect spot, and referred to the Wonderworker as "this thaumaturgic
remedy" (722) — the Greek *thaumaturgos* means "working wonders." As for
the technical terms which snow throughout Ithaca in a steady blizzard,
they read like the speech of a demented impostor at a scientific convention
trying to convince the gathering that he is one of the *cognoscenti*. In short,
no one interested in words can read this episode without laughter.

One of Ithaca's most effective sources of humor is sudden anti-climax.
Every so often, usually just after some lengthy, impressive passage, Joyce
brings everything to a ridiculous halt with a very short, very mundane
answer. After a serious, detailed description of the thermodynamics
involved in bringing water to a boil, this question appears:

> For what personal purpose could Bloom have applied the water so boiled?
>
> To shave himself. (674)

Again, after an elaborate comparison of the Gaelic and Hebrew languages
Bloom solemnly begins to chant the Ha-Tikvah, the Israelitic anthem, but
suddenly stops — "In consequence of defective mnemotechnic" (689). Joyce
twice uses Bloom's cat to achieve this sort of farcical collapse. In the midst
of sentimental reflections on Milly's growing up and leaving home, Bloom
perceives "A temporary departure of his cat" (693), and immediately
following Bloom and Stephen's ritualistically inflated exit from the house
comes this flat tire:

> For what creature was the door of egress a door of ingress?
>
> For a cat. (698)

Not nearly so obvious as Ithaca's humor, and far more subjective, is
its emotional force. Harry Levin, for example, missed this entirely: "There
is no leeway for nostalgia. . . . Instead of emotions, [Joyce] records statistics about the Dublin water-supply; instead of sensations, data about the
conductivity of heat along a spoon."[31] Actually, nostalgia, emotions, and
sensations are vibrantly present. With the possible exception of Molly's
soliloquy, Ithaca unleashes an emotional force more powerful than that of
any other episode in *Ulysses*. And the astonishing intensity of this emotion
is paradoxically attributable directly to the very coldness and objectivity
which, for most readers, seem automatically to exclude any emotion whatever. It is just because events or topics are treated with such baldness that

they assume such poignancy. Consider Bloom's valentine poem to Molly, written shortly before they were married:

> What acrostic upon the abbreviation of his first name had he (kinetic poet) sent to Miss Marion Tweedy on the 14 February 1888?

> **P**oets oft have sung in rhyme
> **O**f music sweet their praise devine.
> **L**et them hymn it nine times nine.
> **D**earer far than song or wine,
> **Y**ou are mine. The world is mine. (678)

That last line, set down without comment by the indifferent artist, is painfully pathetic in the light of Bloom's subsequent relations with Molly and the events of the present day. The same ironic pathos invests the occasion, also just before Bloom's marriage, when he watched the sunrise, recalled now as he stands alone in the darkness of his garden:

> What prospect of what phenomena inclined him to remain?

> The disparition of three final stars, the diffusion of daybreak, the apparition of a new solar disk.

> Had he ever been a spectator of those phenomena?

> Once, in 1887 after a protracted performance of charades in the house of Luke Doyle, Kimmage, he had awaited with patience the apparition of the diurnal phenomenon, seated on a wall, his gaze turned in the direction of Mizrach, the east. (705)

Molly was present at this party and Bloom was very much aware of her ("She leaned on the sideboard watching. Moorish eyes." [377]). Thus the objective description in Ithaca actually presents, with the sudden emotional tug of an old snapshot, a picture of the young Bloom in love with Molly and too excited to sleep. But now, in the early hours of June 17, 1904, seventeen years later, Bloom does not wait for sunrise.

The more emotion a subject inherently possesses, the more cold-blooded is Joyce's objectivity, and the consequent contrast can sometimes be almost brutal. Among the family mementos in the table drawer, for example, is a childish letter of Milly's. Not only has Bloom carefully saved this scrap for years, but he, and the reader, cannot help contrasting its utter ingenuousness with the disturbing significance of the letter Bloom received the previous morning, in which Milly, now 15, casually mentions, "There is a young student comes here some evenings" (66). All this assumes almost overwhelming emotional force as Joyce quotes the childish letter with cold bibliographical precision: "an infantile epistle, dated, small em monday, reading: capital pee Papli comma capital aitch How are you note of interrogation capital eye I am very well full stop new paragraph signature with flourishes capital em Milly no stop" (721).

In addition to its current of intense emotion, Ithaca is subjective in other ways. It is something of a shock to realize that in this apparently most objective of episodes the stream-of-consciousness technique often resides just beneath the surface. Joyce changes the direct discourse of the interior monologue to the indirect discourse of the scientific reporter, but the disguise is frequently very thin. What else, for example, is the following passage but the liquid flow of the stream of consciousness frozen into hard ice?

> What reflections occupied his mind during the process of reversion of the inverted volumes?
>
> The necessity of order, a place for everything and everything in its place: the deficient appreciation of literature possessed by females: the incongruity of an apple incuneated in a tumbler and of an umbrella inclined in a closestool: the insecurity of hiding any secret document behind, beneath or between the pages of a book. (709)

If, as an experiment, and with apologies to the master, we "melt" this passage, the stream will flow again:

> He righted the inverted books. Hate things out of order. Place for everything and everything in its place. No regard for books, literature. Women can't appreciate. No logic. Molly that apple in tumbler, umbrella in closestool. Bad job to hide for instance her letter in book, between books. Think everything safe. Wife dusts. Peekaboo.

The short, elliptical phrases of Joyce's rough notes for Ithaca themselves often resemble elements of the stream of consciousness. The notes for the above question are "place for everything," "LB hates apple in glass," and "Somthg behind books." And occasionally the stream bubbles in small springs through the episode's "dry rocks" surface, emerging clear and unrestricted. In the questions where Stephen relates his Queen's Hotel epiphany (684), and where Bloom recalls phrases from his father's suicide note (723) and lapses into his Sinbad-the-Sailor jumble as he falls asleep (737), the stream of consciousness is in full effect.

There is more of the stream technique in Ithaca, however, than the actual or veiled presentation of snatches of thought. The major stimulus of this technique is free association: a character's reverie flits back and forth among subjects, time and space as this evokes that, now recalls then, here suggests there. And Ithaca is constructed largely on this associational pattern. Again and again one question will trigger another. When Bloom considers the difference between his and Stephen's ages, he is reminded that he met him twice before, once when Stephen was five and again when he was ten. This past connection in turn produces the fact that they both knew Mrs. Riordan, and evokes memories of her eccentricities. The whole discussion of the past, childhood and youth causes Bloom to wonder if he might not once more try "to achieve the rejuvenation" promised by Sandow's indoor exercises, and he muses on his youthful agility on the parallel bars in high school. And so on. The book on the Russo-Turkish War makes him try to remember the name of Plevna; church bells remind him of Dignam's funeral, and that death reminds him of other lost friends; the Queen's Hotel story instantly brings up suicide. Sometimes these associations are not so obvious, but they are usually there. The idea of using essays for entertainment on long winter evenings, for example, is all that is needed to spark an eight-question section on "What to do with our wives." Or again, Bloom's discovery of a forgotten coin in his waistcoat pocket immediately produces the imperative, almost agonized, "Compile the budget for 16 June 1904."

The appearance of cold detachment in Ithaca, then, is betrayed by the reality of constant humor, intense emotion, and disguised stream of consciousness complete with free association. Another betrayal, obvious enough but often overlooked or discounted, is the fact that Ithaca's language is of course frequently anything but "scientific" or even pseudo-scientific. The passages noted above when the stream of consciousness flows in full view are examples. In addition, the many quotations of various documents, however authoritative and accurate they may strive to be, are nevertheless couched in language and invested with a tone entirely non-Ithacan. Thus quotations like the Wonderworker advertisement, Bloom's newspaper poem and acrostic verse to Molly, the 113th Psalm, and others, are brief but definite departures from the technicalities of science. And sometimes Joyce will allow his language to approach poetry, as in "The heaventree of stars hung with humid nightblue fruit" (698), or in the description of Bloom's "melonsmellonous" adoration of Molly's rump (734–35).

Poetic examples like these last two lead to still another quality belying the appearance of cold matter-of-factness. This is rhythm. Ithaca pulses with rhythms throughout, from short passages that are positively metrical to broader rhythms that surge with sweep and fall through extended series of questions. For short toe-tapping rhythms, often employing the onomatopoetic effects Joyce so loved, consider the following:

> The sound of the peal of the hour of the night by the chime of the bells in the church of Saint George. (704)

> A child renamed Padney Socks she shook with shocks her moneybox. (693)

...pedestrians, quadrupeds, velocipedes, vehicles, passing slowly, quickly, evenly, round and round and round the rim of a round precipitous globe. (681)

...a paper read, reread while lathering, relathering the same spot, a shock, a shoot, with thought of aught he sought though fraught with nought might cause a faster rate of shaving and a nick. (674)

Far more subtle, and more difficult both for Joyce to achieve and his reader to recognize, are the cumulative, interactive rhythms which sometimes inform an entire question. An oral reading of the "water hymn," for instance, reveals that Joyce has not just indiscriminately reeled out a monotonous string of facts. Like their subject, the phrases ebb and flow, heave and swell, gather and break, until they subside into the calm quiescence of the concluding "pestilential fens, faded flowerwater, stagnant pools in the waning moon." Many other questions are constructed with similar rhythmical intricacy; outstanding examples are the passage noting the affinities between the moon and woman, a little poem in itself (702), and that describing Bloom as a sun-governed comet ("Ever he would wander..." [727–28]).

The balance examined earlier, both of parallelism and antithesis, with which Joyce repeatedly links two or more questions ("What selfimposed enigma...," "What selfinvolved enigma...," "What selfevident enigma..." [729]), contributes greatly to the rhythms of Ithaca. But there exists a still broader, more sweeping rhythmical pattern, more sensed than seen, involving whole groups of questions and operating in cyclical crescendo and diminuendo throughout the entire episode. This pattern is not easily demonstrable, becoming apparent only through the familiarity of repeated readings. One of its keys is the recurrent use of anti-climax, discussed earlier as a source of humor. After comparatively long-winded or serious or emotional sections, Joyce lets fall one of those short, startlingly abrupt and blunt, and always funny questions. The mood breaks, tension drains, a new subject appears, and another series recommences the upward spiral. But perhaps the best way to perceive and appreciate these varying rhythms is to regard the individual questions of Ithaca as notes in a musical score. Some are short and staccato ("Was the clown Bloom's son? No. Had Bloom's coin returned? Never." [696]), some produce melodic triplets ("Such as?" "Such as not?" "Such as never?" [683–84]), some combine to form progressive chords ("Envy?" "Jealousy?" "Abnegation?" "Equanimity?" "Why more abnegation than jealousy, less envy than equanimity?" [732–33]), and some—those long hypnotic catalogues, widely spaced throughout the composition, carefully led up to and awesomely sustained—are like the climactic high note of Simon Dedalus' song in the Ormond bar, "everywhere all soaring all around about the all, the endlessnessnessness..." (276).

"This frightful text," one can now see, is really two texts. In full, glaring view is the immediate foreground, where all is, or appears to be, analytical, scientific, naturalistic, and indifferent, and yet actually amounts to massive parody of these same qualities. But there is also a more or less inconspicuous hinterland, where all is humorous, touching, subjective, and rhythmical. Bluntness thus masks subtlety, and there exists a continuous interplay between the two. One will succeed the other, producing sudden contrasts, or, more often, both will function simultaneously, growing out of and intensifying each other. And this dualism in structure, style and tone, where the forbidding and the attractive are interdependent, is also manifest in the matter of theme.

5

The Theme of
Isolation and Community

Confronted with Ithaca, one mystified critic complained, "...this massive accumulation, this enormous *stasis,* is presented to us at a point where we suppose ourselves to be moving towards the resolution of a fable. What, we ask, is this resolution? The mountain has laboured. But where is the mouse?"[1]

Thus readers who make their way past the four technical or stylistic barriers of interrogative method, science, naturalism, and indifference can be brought up short before a fifth and more forbidding barrier, that of theme. What does everything add up to? What does Ithaca *mean*? And since this episode is the culmination, the last eventful chapter of the novel, this question really becomes, what does *Ulysses* mean? Stephen and Bloom, their paths intersecting all day, have met, have talked, have parted. One knows what they have said, but what has Joyce said?

Critical interpretations of *Ulysses* often split into two antithetical groups. On the one side is the view that the book has, to use a convenient label, an unhappy ending. According to this view, the lives of Stephen, Bloom and Molly are hopeless failures, filled with frustration, incompatibility and loneliness. The central theme here is total defeat. Directly opposed to this is the happy ending view: the meeting of Stephen and Bloom, under the beneficent influence of Molly, produces, or at least makes possible, self-determination, reconciliation and salvation. All here is complete or potential success. One of the "Invitation to Learning" radio programs thirty years after the novel's publication was exemplary of those two views. William G. Rogers, literary editor of the Associated Press, and Professor William York Tindall summed up the book like this:

> Rogers: "...it seems to me that we have two men who are as dissatisfied at heart in the end as they were at the beginning, two men whose ideals are no closer to realization after seven hundred and fifty pages than they were on page

one. That is why I think a book written in what is fundamentally a comic mood has a very depressing and tragic conclusion."

Tindall: "It is a comedy. There is no doubt about that. But I think it's a comedy in the sense that Dante's *Divine Comedy* is one. That is, it's a success story.... It's a book of great acceptance and, I think, joy."[2]

Tragedy—comedy. Failure—success. Which is "true"? Which was Joyce's intention? For the sake of amicability, critics who argue this dilemma, whichever side they are on, usually conclude by generously agreeing that such disagreement just shows how great a novel *Ulysses* is. While this may preserve the peace, it also preserves the dilemma.

The present study contends that both views, failure and success, are demonstrably valid, that they are not mutually exclusive but essentially interdependent, and that Joyce presents the central theme of the novel through the inextricable union of the two. We may first examine the two interpretations separately, to establish the disturbing fact that they are both indisputably justified, and then we shall be able—indeed, forced—to consider the significance of their co-existence.

It has long been recognized that *Ulysses* is a fusion of two literary methods, naturalism and symbolism, and therefore operates basically on two levels: a naturalistic surface of definite events and a symbolic subsurface of indefinite suggestions. Failure dominates the naturalistic level, success the symbolic level. Examining what first claims attention, the surface, Harry Levin saw Ithaca like this: "The decision of this indecisive day is for each of them to continue—Stephen as an exile, Bloom as a Dubliner.... With every futile question and perfunctory reply, they become more aware of the barriers that separate them.... Their lives are related only by the widest generalities or the most extraneous details.... Bloom has nothing to offer Stephen but a pathetic object-lesson.... Both are at sea, helpless among the cross-currents of contemporary life."[3]

Evidence supporting this view appears abundantly throughout Ithaca. The incompatibility of Stephen and Bloom has already been strongly emphasized in the preceding Eumaeus episode, where Stephen yawns in Bloom's face, often talks over his head when he talks at all, insults him rudely ("We can't change the country. Let us change the subject" [645]), obviously accepts the proposal to go to Bloom's house out of sheer apathy, and even feels a physical repulsion when Bloom takes his arm ("...he felt a strange kind of flesh of a different man approach him, sinewless and wobbly..." [666]). By the time they reach 7 Eccles Street, Stephen has revived sufficiently to become more sociable. They discuss the past, compare languages, and even sing songs (though not together). But no real change has occurred. Bloom still carries the conversation, sometimes almost desperately. There are long pauses. The host still does not understand many of his guest's remarks, and disagrees with much that he does grasp (literature, for example, is not an "eternal affirmation of the spirit of man" [666]). The sixteen-year gap in their ages is forever unbridgeable (679). Bloom knows that Stephen knows that Bloom is a Jew, and both avoid mention of the fact (681–82); they represent antithetical temperaments —"The scientific. The artistic" (683). And finally, of course, there is Stephen's refusal to stay the night in Bloom's house: he declines the invitation "with amicability, gratefully," but also "promptly, inexplicably" (695). It is, in effect, a pleasant but decisive "Thanks, but no thanks." Nearly 700 pages have prepared for a meeting which ends in separation. Nothing has been achieved, nothing has come to fruition. Standing solitary in his garden, Bloom now feels only the "lonechill" of the "cold of interstellar space" (704).

Chilly as all this may be, other considerations are even colder. Stephen and Bloom not only fail to achieve any real companionship, they also fail to overcome their own individual problems. Homeless Stephen has achieved no solution to his deep-rooted obsessions, and no alteration is apparent in his deficiencies of character and outlook. He is still proud, arrogant, semi-neurotic; he has not given up his moody brooding; he has not awakened from the nightmare which is history; he is still afflicted with "Agenbite of inwit." Significantly, the last glimpse of Stephen's mind reveals the same guilt-ridden conscience that has tortured him since the first episode: in the bells of St. George's Church, tolling as he leaves Bloom, he hears the prayer (*"Liliata rutilantium. . . ."* [704]) which he associates with his mother's death. As for Bloom, left alone, the remainder of Ithaca, more than thirty pages, is one long testimonial of his ineffectuality and loneliness. He has not got his Keyes advertisement; the utopian vision of Agendath Netaim literally goes up in flames (707); he must salve his failures with reveries of success and rationalize his cuckoldry into a comfortable "equanimity" (733). Falling asleep among whirling transformations of Sinbad the Sailor, he is still the Wandering Jew, and "Ever he would wander. . ." (727). His relations with Molly remain sterile; for him an advantage of "an occupied, as distinct from an unoccupied bed" (728) is the economy of mangling his trousers beneath the mattress under her weight.

All this and more forms the foundation for the tragic-ending view. And this interpretation, considered as a whole, is perfectly sound. The theory that *Ulysses* is not a success story is fundamentally unassailable; an attempt to disprove it is certain to founder in the waves of plain evidence. If, however, instead of assaulting the failure theory, one searches for evidence of success, he will discover the apparent impossibility that it too is not only present but is equally unassailable. This magic trick is accomplished by mirrors—the mirrors of symbolism. If Ithaca is examined not as naturalistic narrative but as symbolic suggestion, all is by no means so unhappy as the literal surface insists, for, as David Daiches puts it, the episode "contains all kinds of ritual overtones involving the reconciliation of opposites and the possibility of sacramental identification of oneself with someone else."[4]

In this shadowy realm of implication almost everything in Ithaca is the opposite of the hard, literal surface, with its failure, loneliness, and incompatibility. Here, on the other hand, are repeated suggestions of acceptance, union, and sublimation. Stephen finds a "father" in Bloom, and thereby moves toward stability and self-determination; Bloom gains a "son" in Stephen, and his lonely life assumes new significance. As Stephen wanders off to fulfill his destiny, Bloom turns to his proper place—home and Molly. Moses has reached the promised land, Sinbad has made port, and the Wandering Jew, who "has travelled," now "rests" (737). The doxology of Molly's soliloquy sounds a majestic alleluia, her final "Yes" a fervent amen.

It cannot be too strongly emphasized that Joyce does not "say" all this, that one cannot point to this or that place in the text and "prove," for example, that Stephen accepts Bloom as a father. Joycean symbolism does not work that way. It works by suggestion, by accumulation of significant ambiguities, by contextual relationships. It is an invitation, not a declaration. Failure to understand this has moved some critics to contemptuous denunciation of symbolic interpretation. On the other hand, it should be remembered that symbolism itself is a delicate business, containing the seeds of its own corruption. The danger is over-interpretation—reading in meanings, forcing conclusions, ignoring proper context. Assigning symbolic value arbitrarily, critics sometimes deserve reproof for engaging in what has been called "playing the game of 'hunt the symbol.'"

The validity of symbolic interpretation, however, should not in the general censure take corruption from this particular fault. The fact remains that Ithaca is shot through with a symbolism whose implications directly counterpoint the explicit surface. Where the surface, for example, presents futility and failure, the symbolic counterpoint emphasizes a theme of renewal, resurrection, and rebirth. Bloom's table drawer contains a recipe "for renovation of old tan boots" (721), his nightly meditations produce "renovated vitality" (720), and the Wonderworker will make "a new man of you" (722). The schoolfellow slain by the Jew's daughter in Stephen's ballad is resurrected when Bloom, inviting Stephen to stay the night, envisages a "union between a schoolfellow and a jew's daughter" (695). We are told "of moribund and of nascent new stars such as Nova in 1901" (698), of "a new luminous sun generated by the collision. . .of two nonluminous exsuns," and of "the new moon with the old moon in her arms" (700). Stephen's departure through the gate (with its "female lock" unlocked by a "male key" 703) becomes parturition; Bloom in "his cometary orbit" will "reappear reborn" (728), and in bed he is "the manchild in the womb" (737). There are many other such references.

Supporting and enlarging this theme of renewal is the theme of darkness and light, two qualities that alternate and contrast throughout Ithaca like death and life. Bloom shows Stephen both in and out of the dark house with his 1 C P candle and finally, at its extinction, is enlightened about Moses (729). The setting in Stephen's epiphany about the girl writing in the Queen's Hotel is "Twilight. Fire lit" (684). Milly is "blond, born of two dark" (693). Stephen and Bloom emerge "doubly dark, from obscurity. . .into the penumbra of the garden" (698), where they see scintillating stars, a meteor, and Molly's luminous window—lighted by a lamp which casts "varying gradations of light and shadow" (736). After describing the "attendant phenomena of eclipses" (701), Joyce describes, in parallel phrases, the "initial paraphenomena" of daybreak (705). And Bloom's last semi-conscious thought before sleep is of "Darkinbad the Brightdayler" (737).

Attention to such recurrent motifs is certainly not "playing the game of 'hunt the symbol.'" Present in force, they require no hunting; accumulations like these cannot be dismissed. One may argue over the interpretation of this or that phrase, but there can be no argument that, taken as a whole, Ithaca's symbolism portends optimistic promise. Joyce's rough notes provide additional testimony. Litz has called attention to an entry in one of the notesheets for the Eumaeus episode, "UL & Tel exchange unity."[5] Ulysses and Telemachus exchange little enough unity in Eumaeus, to be sure, but they begin the Ithaca episode by "Starting united. . . ." Among the Ithaca notesheets, though, is perhaps the single most significant entry of all Joyce's notes: "SD will win else LB wdn't." Stephen's success will automatically be Bloom's, for it is Bloom who makes it possible. On the victory of the son depends the victory of the father: "He saw in a quick young male familiar form the predestination of a future" (689).

Enough has been said to show that both the theme of failure and the theme of success are unquestionably present in Ithaca. The result would seem to be logically impossible and critically intolerable; black is white and white is black. The reader, in short, is presented with a negative affirmative. No wonder much Joycean criticism tries to argue one theme or the other out of existence. Together they invite chaos. Nevertheless, only when the fact is accepted that they are there, and that neither can be argued away or ignored, can the dilemma be resolved. Here are two divisions of one theme: the theme of isolation and community. Joyce has presented his view of the human condition: isolation striving for community. The surface of Ithaca sets forth the brutal fact of human isolation. Man in his physical universe is separate, insular, alone, tragically imprisoned in the solitary confinement of the self. But physical isolation, far from precluding spiritual community, is the very cause of man's search for sodality. And the symbolic subsurface of Ithaca presents man's strong desire for community and proclaims the possibility of its occasional and temporary achievement. An isolated creature, man is at least together with others who are alone; at most, he can under rare and tenuous circumstances transcend his singularity and enter into joyous, if pathetically brief, communion with kindred spirits.

Joyce took special care that Ithaca, his culminating episode, should sound, echo, and re-echo, through both symbolic suggestion and direct statement, the theme of isolation and community. Repeated references to it embroider the very first page. The "parallel course" of the opening words is a perfect inaugural statement of the theme: Stephen and Bloom are separate but together. Key phrases in the opening questions develop this idea. Displaying "like and unlike reactions," the two men are, on the one hand, a "duumvirate" who start out "united" and share "common factors of similarity," but they are also, on the other hand, "disparate" and possess "divergent" views. The first question, and many others throughout the episode, plays significantly on the words "both" and "each." And except for the words "similarity" and "divergent," every one of these terms was inserted as an individual addition in typescript or proofs, right down to "both" and "each." Even the two exceptions were parts of questions added to the basic manuscript. Throughout his different drafts, therefore, one can watch Joyce carefully planting the seeds of his theme, as he adds "united," "like and unlike," "common factors," and "disparate" to the typescript, "parallel" and "both" and "each" to the galley proof, and "duumvirate" to the page proof.

Having presented the theme so strongly at the beginning, Joyce is also careful to emphasize it when Bloom and Stephen bid farewell. As they stand on "different sides" of the "same door," their hands meet in "union" and part in "disunion" while "both and each" hear the chimes of St. George's Church (703–4). These terms were not individual additions, but the questions in which they appear were added late in composition.

Joyce does not depend solely on such veiled revelation, however, for presenting the theme of isolation and community. He brings it explicitly to the surface. Bloom, walking to Eccles Street with Stephen, remembers other times when he made similar "nocturnal perambulations," and reflects that the older one grows the lonelier one becomes, or, in the language of Ithaca:

> He reflected that the progressive extension of the field of individual development and experience was regressively accompanied by a restriction of the converse domain of interindividual relations.
>
> As in what ways?
>
> From inexistence to existence he came to many and was as one received: existence with existence he was with any as any with any: from existence to nonexistence gone he would be by all as none perceived. (667–68)

Both questions are explicit, if ludicrously involved, statements of the theme, and both questions are additions to the galley proof. Or again, consider Stephen and Bloom beneath Molly's window:

> Both then were silent?
>
> Silent, each contemplating the other in both mirrors of the reciprocal flesh of theirhisnothis fellowfaces. (702)

This question is present in the basic manuscript, but lacking the important words "reciprocal" and "theirhisnothis," which were added in proof. The compressed "theirhisnothis" (Joyce first wrote it as "his nothis") is a striking nutshell expression of the theme. A final example is what Bloom sees in his mirror. In the manuscript he sees only "The image of a solitary man," but Joyce later expanded this to read, "The image of a solitary (ipsorelative) mutable (aliorelative) man" (708). Ipsorelatively, Bloom is alone, monadic, egocentric; aliorelatively, he is, simply, Everyman. Ipso-alio Bloom is simultaneously self and other, each and every, one and all.

Readers of *Ulysses* are sometimes put off because they feel Joyce does not say anything: he may adorn a tale, but where does he point a moral? Joyce had no intention of "saying" anything. He told Frank Budgen, after learning that some readers were dissatisfied with the way *Ulysses* was progressing in its serial publication, "They seem to think that after writing *A Portrait* I should have sat down to write something like a sermon. I ought to have a message, it seems."[6] The theme of isolation and community is not a message. It is the disclosure of a perception of man's position among men and in his universe.

6

An Ithacan Glossary

Any episode of *Ulysses* contains so closely woven a pattern of motifs, symbols, allusions, autobiographical connections, cross-references to other episodes, and so forth, that an attempt to separate and classify all of them for study would be more confusing than enlightening. Instead, many points of interest are better dealt with as they appear in the chronology of the text. The following glossary (the term is used in its widest sense), taking things as they come, presents a page-by-page survey of Ithaca, a running commentary ranging from suggestion to explanation.[1] Particular attention is paid to the relationship between Joyce's rough notes and the text, and to the significance of revisions made during the various stages of composition.

One matter, however, is bettter dealt with right here, and that is Joyce's schema of technique, art, symbol and organ for Ithaca. This sort of structural apparatus, most Joyceans now agree, was of far more importance to the author than it has subsequently been to his readers. Scholastic, methodical Joyce loved to erect such a scaffolding, and it was primarily his own ostentatious secrecy about the whole business (and Stuart Gilbert's overemphasis when Joyce selected him for the authorized revelation), rather than any intrinsic value, that elevated the schema to an undeserved and misleading position of vital importance. A brief review here will suffice for Ithaca. The "technique" of impersonal catechism, of course, counterpoints the personal catechism of the Nestor episode. Just as there Stephen first questions the schoolboys and then is questioned by Mr. Deasy, so here Bloom first questions Stephen and then is questioned by Molly. The "art" of science and "symbol" of comets are clear enough. The skeleton as "organ" probably applies to the episode's extreme objectivity: all flesh of sentiment or feeling is stripped away, leaving only the hard, bare bones for cold inspection.[2]

666: Mention of "gaslight or the light of arc and glowlamps" begins the motif of light, which shines throughout the episode with candles, lucifer matches, firelight, Mrs. Riordan's colza oil lamp, moonlight, rising sun, Molly's lamp and other manifestations.

667: Bloom has thought of Cormac earlier: "That last pagan king of Ireland Cormac in the schoolpoem choked himself at Sletty southward of the Boyne" (169). The "schoolpoem" is Samuel Ferguson's "The Burial of King Cormac," which contains the lines

> He choked upon the food he ate,
> At Sletty, southward of the Boyne.[3]

668: It is now well known that 7 Eccles Street was the residence of Joyce's friend, J. F. Byrne ("Cranly" in *A Portrait*), who entered the house one keyless night through the front area. According to Ellmann, Bloom's height is that of Byrne, and his weight is that registered for Byrne on a penny scale that same night.[4] If so, the weight at least gave Joyce's memory some trouble: Bloom is first eleven stone and four onces (manuscript), then ten stone and four pounds (galley proof), and finally the present eleven stone and four pounds (page proof). The drop into the area is part of the resurrection motif: "Did he fall?" and "Did he rise...?" are underscored by mention of the "feast of the Ascension."

669: "MXMIV," which should be MCMIV, is the first of a number of mathematical errors in Ithaca. Joyce was no mathematician (Stephen at Clongowes Wood: "He was no good at sums but he tried his best." *A Portrait,* 12). Joyce's difficulties, in typescript and proofs, in reaching correct totals for Bloom's budget (711) are something to behold. The "lighted crevice of doorway" introduces the presence of Molly, and Joyce is careful to keep her "present" during the conversation of Stephen and Bloom: her stockings hang before Stephen's eyes, her cream is sacrificed for the cocoa, her Italian and singing lessons are discussed, and so on.

670: Brother Michael and Father Butt appear in *A Portrait,* Kate and Julia Morkan in "The Dead." The addresses listed for the Dedalus family are two of the many Dublin addresses of the Joyce family. After the list of firebuilders, the manuscript contains the following question, cancelled in typescript when Joyce developed the later question on the ages of Bloom and Stephen (678):

> What did Bloom think of their different ages?

> That neither could Stephen now have his age then nor he then Stephen's now.

671: According to R. M. Adams, "the whole latter half of the description of the Dublin waterworks...comes from a letter to the Irish Independent written by Ignatius J. Rice, and published in the issue of June 15,

1904."⁵ Concerning the South Dublin Guardians and paupers: "The South Dublin Poor Law Union was an administrative grouping of the municipal wards of Dublin for which a separate poor rate was struck and administered by an elected body of Poor Law Guardians."⁶ Bloom's admiration of water, the first of the episode's half-dozen lengthy catalogues, is perhaps the most remarkable single passage in Ithaca. Hugh Kenner praises its achievement of "the improbable feat of raising to poetry all the clutter of footling information that has accumulated in schoolbooks."⁷ Here is the culmination of the water motif in *Ulysses* (but not the end, for water is prominent in Molly's soliloquy). Along with other liquids, such as tea, urine, milk and cream, Guinness's porter, and Bass's ale, water is a vital part of the novel's vast theme of everlasting, everchanging life. The "hole in the wall" was the name of a pub near the Ashtown Gate on the north side of Dublin's Phoenix Park.⁶ The "potentiality derivable from harnessed tides of watercourses falling from level to level," as well as water's "docility in working hydraulic millwheels, turbines, dynamos, electric power stations," reappears later as one of Bloom's schemes for wealth (718).

672: As Bloom washes his hands, that famous cake of soap makes its final appearance. Joyce's laconic note is simply "Soap useful."

674: The "masculine feminine" nature of Bloom's hand continues the motif of Bloom as epicene, prominent throughout *Ulysses* (cf. the Wonderworker prospectus addressed to "Mrs. L. Bloom...commencing Dear Madam" (721).

675: The "chipped eggcup containing pepper" in the kitchen dresser suggests the incomplete, sterile relationship of the Blooms, as does the "empty pot of Plumtree's potted meat," without which, of course, home is incomplete. The purpose of the "phial of aromatic violet comfits" is revealed in Molly's soliloquy: "I hope my breath was sweet after those kissing comfits" (770). The potted meat, fruit and wine were sent to Molly by Blazes Boylan, who told the shopgirl, "It's for an invalid" (227): hence the wordplay here on "invalid port."

676: Bloom's "previous intimations of the result" of the Gold Cup race form the first of several recapitulations in Ithaca of events occurring earlier in the day. Others appear when Bloom compiles his budget (711), recalls the causes of his fatigue (728–29), and narrates his adventures to Molly (735).

677: A notesheet entry reveals that Joyce originally intended Bloom to read Newman, not Shakespeare: "he read J. H. N. for solution of difficulty—disappointed."

678: The names Joyce lists for the *Sinbad the Sailor* pantomime were, with one exception, the actual people in the performance. (See the accompanying reproduction of the program for the opening performance on

December 26, 1892. The original is in the National Library of Ireland. Joyce, however, apparently got his information not from this program, but from an advertisement in the *Freeman's Journal* for December 24 and 26, 1892, since he includes some names present in the ad but not in the program.[8]) The exception is "Nelly Bouverist, principal girl," whose non-intellectual, non-political, non-topical" face and underclothing distracted Bloom. Among the cast, however, was Nellie Bouverie, to whose name Joyce apparently added the final syllable of the name of Kate Neverist, also in the cast. (With this change, Joyce was probably guarding against possible libel action. As a "non-intellectual" and an exhibitor of "white articles of...underclothing," the real Nellie Bouverie would have a fine case.) When Joyce added this question to the first typescript, he used the name "Fay Arthur" instead of "Nelly Bouverist," probably having some fun at the expense of the actors William and Frank Fay and Arthur Sinclair. If so, he had second thoughts during galley-proof revision, when he decided to spotlight poor Nelly. The pantomime's "Tinbad (the Tailor)" and "Whinbad (the Whaler)" also shows us where Joyce got the idea for Bloom's sleepy whirl of alliterative Sinbads at the end of Ithaca (737). Sinbad is not only a Ulysses-Bloom surrogate with his travels and adventures (in one he blinds a one-eyed giant), but he is also a Daedalus figure, for he twice escapes from predicaments by contriving to have a large bird fly away with him. Joyce, incidentally, owned the seventeen-volume Burton translation of *The Arabian Nights.*

679: By carrying their ages into past and future, Joyce gives Stephen and Bloom archetypal stature. As several commentators have noted, however, Joyce himself is carried away by his mathematics: the last two figures should be 20,230 and 17,158, not 83,300 and 81,396.

680: The phrasing here of Bloom's refusing the young Stephen's dinner invitation parallels Stephen's refusal of Bloom's invitation to stay overnight. About Mrs. Riordan and the City Arms Hotel: after the fight about Parnell dramatized in the famous Christmas dinner scene in *A Portrait,* she left the Dedalus/Joyce house for the safety of the hotel.

681: The spectacle of "a round precipitous globe" seen through "a rondel of bossed glass" contains both macrocosm and microcosm.

682: With a maternal grandmother who was "born Hegarty," Bloom is apparently one-quarter Irish. The observation on the "university of life" was made by Bloom during the courtroom scene in Circe (459).

683: In his notes Joyce carefully reproduced the twelve signs of the zodiac from Aries to Pisces.

684: Ellmann writes that Rudolph Bloom's death "is made to take place at the Queen's Hotel in Ennis because Joyce remembered a suicide that occurred there early in the century."[9]

685: Joyce himself wrote a school essay on Ulysses entitled "My Favourite Hero." His note for this passage reads, "To SD publish Maunsel school essays Si. D. read out as models." Doctor Dick has not been exactly identified, but Heblon was a pseudonym for Joseph K. O'Connor; both were commercial writers in Dublin, Dick specializing in occasional verse and Heblon in a kind of slum-life, police-court journalism. The point is that they here join Philip Beaufoy in Bloom's mind as artistic models.

686: The whole section on "What to do with our wives," perhaps the funniest in Ithaca, deals with a subject about which Joyce had some convictions. He told Frank Budgen that Christ was not a perfect man because he had never lived with a woman, explaining that "Surely living with a woman is one of the most difficult things a man has to do."[10] Joyce built up this section carefully in his notes, recording entries like the following:

> MB bored at night (play draughts)
> play duets with MB
> scrivenry—add env. for MB [i.e., addressing envelopes]
> Put Molly in dairy
> Brothels for women save trouble
> MB wrote Greek
> MB believed Alias was somebody in the scriptures
> LB leaves book open purposely
> Molly takes umbrella if good hat

687: Moses Maimonides (1135–1204)—Jewish philosopher and master of rabbinical literature. Moses Mendelssohn (1729–1786)—German-Jewish philosopher and champion of Jewish emancipation, grandfather of the composer Felix. "Mendoza (pugilist)"—Daniel Mendoza, an English Jew, who flourished in the ring about 1790. Ferdinand Lassalle (1825–1864)—German-Jewish labor reformer and socialist, whose love affair and fatal duel form the subject of Meredith's *The Tragic Comedians*. The ridiculous incongruity of the prizefighter's presence among Mendelssohn, Spinoza and Lassalle is typical of Bloom and Ithaca.

688: Concerning the antiquity of Hebrew, a notesheet entry observes "Hebrew dead language in Jesus time." Fenius Farsaigh, the legendary inventor of the ogham character, is said to have established an academy of languages on the Plain of Shinar, where he cultivated the Gaelic dialect which, via Phoenician traders, traveled to Spain and thence to Ireland.[11] Heber and Heremon were brother Milesian chieftains: in *Finnegans Wake* they become "Hebear and Hairyman." The Book of the Dun Cow, Book of Ballymote, and Garland of Howth are, like the famous book of Kells, early manuscripts; the first is so named from the color of the hide from which its vellum was made.

"THE SHIP HOTEL, Lr. Abbey Street, can vie with any

HYAM'S New Goods for the Winter Season have arrived GENTLEMEN will find the 42 - OVERCOATS equal in value to any sold elsewhere at 55   They are made from IRISH TWEEDS, CHEVIOTS, DIAGONAL COATINGS, BEAVERS, NAPS, MELTONS, &c, the value of which will astonish all who see them.

The Quality and Finish of HYAMS of last Winter were generally admitted to be superior to any obtainable elsewhere at much higher prices, notwithstanding which, the value being given for this season's OVERCOATS greatly excels that of last year.

42/- OVERCOATS MADE TO ORDER

29 and 30, DAME STREET, DUBLIN

DRINK

SHANKS'S

HOP

BITTERS.

THE GREAT

TEMPERANCE

BEVERAGE.

Sold in

TYOSDA

and

GAIETY

BARS.

MARKS BROS.,
HOUSE ✦ PAINTERS ✦ AND ✦ DECORATORS,
South Anne Street.
MODERATE CHARGES.
FIRST CLASS WORK.

MONDAY, DECEMBER 26th, 1892.

At One, and Evening at Eight.

The Grand Christmas Pantomime,

SINDBAD THE SAILOR

CHARACTERS.

Mrs. Eliza Sindbad		...	Mr. T. W. VOLT
Sindbad	(the Sailor)		Miss VIOLET EVELYN
Tindbad	(the Tailor)		Mr. WILLIE CRACKLES
Whinbad	(the Whaler)		Miss NELLIE BOUVERIE
Capt. William M'Turco		...	Mr. E. W. LOYCE
The Hon. Horatio Cassawari			Miss ANNIE TEESDALE
Sir William Crosstree			Miss KATHLEEN MORGAN
Lieutenant Mainbrace			Miss MARIE SMITH
Ben Bolstay	(1st Mate)		Mr. WILLIAM OTTO
Jack Marlinspike	(2nd Mate)		Mr. THOMAS OTTO
Sambo	(the Cook)		Mr. FRED OTTO
Shiperwreckeros	(the Demon)		Mr. JESS SMITH
Old Man of the Sea			Little KATIE WALLACE
Rhumphiz	(the Sultan)		Mr. F. J. LITTLE
Zorilda	(Sindbad's Sister)		Miss KATE NEVERIST
Suleyma	(the Princess)		Miss IDA LOGAN
Izra	(her Maid)		Miss DOROTHY DENIS
Oceana	(the Fairy)		Miss MAY HAZLEWOOD

Sailor Boys, Lasses, Merchants, Attendants, Retainers, etc., etc.

FULL BAND, CHORUS & BALLET

THE MARVEL OF THE AGE

LESLIE'S
—OPERA—
VOICE LOZENGES.
A PERFECT CURE
FOR
ALL AFFECTIONS
OF THE
VOICE and THROAT

MDLLE. ZELIE DE LUSSAN.
"Leslie's Opera Voice Lozenges are excellent."
ZELIE DE LUSSAN.
TESTIMONIAL FROM

PRICES IN BOXES—
1/1¼, 2 9, and 4 6 each.
To be had of all Chemists or direct from the Makers and Patentees

P. A. LESLIE & CO
36, Bride St., Dublin
Can now be had at the BARS of the Theatre.

Now Open, **NEARY'S NEW BAR,** 1 Chath
HALF A MIN

SINGER'S BREWING MACHINES, from £3 16s. each, or

Program for the opening performance, December 26, 1892, of the
Sinbad the Sailor pantomime (verso leaf).

Program for the opening performance, December 26, 1892, of the
Sinbad the Sailor pantomime (recto leaf).

689: By signing *Sweets of Sin* Stephen symbolically endorses Molly; Joyce's note reads, "LB gets SD's signature by artifice." Epiphanius the Monk and Johannes Damascenus, or John of Damascus, are saints who lived in the fourth and eighth centuries, but Lentulus the Roman (Publius Lentulus) is, according to both Weldon Thornton and Don Gifford with Robert Seidman, fictitious[12]—legend holds that as governor of Judea preceding Pontius Pilate he sent a letter to the Roman senate describing the physical appearance of Christ. R. M. Adams, however, states that these three figures are "all historical."[13]

690: Vladimir Nabokov writes, "Stephen with his usual detached cruelty recites a little medieval ballad about the Jew's daughter...."[14] But folklorists take note: Stephen's rendition of the "strange legend" of "Little Harry Hughes" is almost certainly a new and authentically Irish version of the famous Hugh of Lincoln ballad. At first thought, it would seem senseless to seek Joyce's source for a story centuries old and extant in many varying forms, including Chaucer's "The Prioress's Tale." But Joyce's referring to the Christian victim as "Harry Hughes" leads the researcher to a fascinating discovery. Consulting Francis James Child's definitive collection of ballads, he finds that only one version, unique in itself, contains this name;[15] all other versions—and Child reproduces nearly twenty—contain the name "Sir Hugh." Whence, then, this singular version? In a volume compiled some years before Child's collection, William Wells Newell has described his surprise at hearing a colored child sing the hitherto unknown "Harry Hughes" variant on a New York City street.[16] The child had learned it from her mother, who in turn had learned it from *her* mother *in Ireland*. The stanzas relevant to Joyce's version are as follows:

> It was on a May, on a midsummer's day,
>   When it rained, it did rain small;
> And little Harry Hughes and his playfellows all
>   Went out to play the ball.
>
> He knocked it up, and he knocked it down,
>   He knocked it oer and oer;
> The very first kick little Harry gave the ball,
>   He broke the duke's windows all.
>
> She came down, the youngest duke's daughter,
>   She was dressed in green:
> 'Come back, come back, my pretty little boy,
>   And play the ball again.'
>
> 'I won't come back, and I daren't come back,
>   Without my playfellows all;

And if my mother she should come in,
   She'd make it the bloody ball.'

She takes him by the lily-white hand,
   And leads him from hall to hall,
Until she came to a little dark room,
   That no one could hear him call.

She sat herself on a golden chair,
   Him on another close by,
And there's where she pulled out her little penknife,
   That was both sharp and fine.

Little Harry Hughes had to pray for his soul,
   For his days were at an end;
She stuck her penknife in little Harry's heart,
   And first the blood came very thick, and then came very thin.

Joyce's ballad, despite its differences, is clearly a close relative to this version; no other given by Child is nearly so similar. And it is virtually certain that Joyce is recalling a song he knew by heart from Dublin days. We know that although the words under the music in the *Ulysses* text were written down by Joyce himself, the musical notation was written by his friend Jacques Benoîst-Méchin,[17] and surely this was done as Joyce sang the song to him, for otherwise Joyce himself would simply have copied the notation from a printed source. (The musical notation transcribed by Newell for the New York version is completely different from Joyce's.) Thus "Little Harry Hughes," a peculiarly Irish version of the ballad, appeared in New York and Paris some forty or more years apart. Joyce's version reveals two major innovations: the unusual and probably corrupt six-line initial stanza, found neither in the New York version nor in any other, and the decapitation of little Harry (in all other versions he is stabbed with the penknife). These may have been present in the Irish song as Joyce knew it, or may be attributable to a hazy memory or deliberate alteration.

   691: The phrase "a jew's daughter, all dressed in green" reads in manuscript "a jew's daughter, Millicent (Milly), all dressed in green." When Joyce, in the typescript, substituted "the father of Millicent" for "the host" in the question, he removed Millicent's name from the answer. This is not the first time Bloom has pondered the subject of this ballad; in Glasnevin cemetery the previous morning he remembered the story in a context stressing resurrection: "It's the blood sinking in the earth gives new life. Same idea those jews they said killed the christian boy" (108).

   693: Thinking of Milly in the Nausicaa episode, Bloom remembers, "Loved to count my waistcoat buttons" (380), and, in Circe, while counting the buckles on Zoe's dress, he lisps, "One two tlee; tlee tlwo tlone," (501). With Milly's "blond ancestry, remote, a violation, Herr Hauptmann Hainau, Austrian army," we see that Bloom's cuckoldry is not without precedent in the Virag family.

695: The "disintegration of obsession" which Stephen's presence might bring about refers to Molly's brooding on Rudy's death. Concerning mother and daughter, a notesheet entry reads, "LB conquered mother by daughter, daught by mother." We are told that Stephen declines Bloom's invitation "promptly," but actually the offer seems to be followed by an embarrassing silence: Stephen's refusal comes five questions after the proposal. Bloom awkwardly tries to bridge the gap with his "inconsequent" question about Mrs. Sinico (her death occurs in "A Painful Case"). One of Joyce's notes suggests that the possibility of interest on Stephen's "loan" really worries Bloom: "SD and the interest?"

696: William Empson argues that since it was Bloom who made the "proposal" to stay overnight, the "counterproposals" here are made by Stephen, and are therefore evidence that he intends to see more of Bloom and to meet Molly.[18] This is most unlikely, entirely out of character and mood for Stephen. These counterproposals are simply Bloom's pathetic alternatives.

697: For the jargonistic phrasing of "catastrophic cataclysms which make terror the basis of human mentality: seismic upheavals the epicentres of which are located in densely populated regions," Joyce's notes read simply "Fear base of life" and "Why earthquakes occur where people are?" With "a micro- and a macrocosm ineluctably constructed upon the incertitude of the void," Stephen is pompously parading for Bloom one of his library-scene thoughts ("the church is founded and founded irremovably because founded, like the world, macro- and microcosm, upon the void. Upon incertitude, upon unlikelihood" [207]). Bloom cannot accept the pessimism: "he, a conscious reactor against the void of incertitude" (734).

698: Explicating the ritualistic exit from the house, William York Tindall is happily in his symbolistic element: "'Diaconal hat': Stephen is still a deacon, not yet a priest, of the imagination. Father Bloom's candle suggests the Mass for Holy Saturday, which, centering on the Paschal Candle, celebrates new light in darkness, enlightenment heralding the morrow (Easter). In this mass (Joyce's favorite) 'the light of Christ' disperses 'the darkness of the whole world,' as God's light guided 'Moses when he went out of Egypt.' A deacon assists at this preparation for renewal. Cf. Stephen's 'introit for paschal time' " (431).[19] The stars pointed out by Bloom suggest symbolic parallels with many of the novel's themes. Sirius, the brightest star in the sky, is not only in Canis Major, but is also the "Dog Star," and so takes its place in the Stephen-dog motif running through

Ulysses (see, for example, the black mass scene in Circe, [599–600]). In ancient times Sirius was associated with both fertility and sterility, life and death. When the Nile was rising, Egyptians regarded Sirius as "a herald of the waters which would overspread the land, renewing its fertility" (*Encyclopaedia Britannica*). To the Greeks, however, the star was a herald of evil, announcing the hot, dry season—its name comes from the Greek *seirios,* "scorching." (While writing *Ulysses* Joyce said, "The word *scorching* has a peculiar significance for my superstitious mind...because...the progress of the book is in fact like the progress of some sandblast." Each succeeding episode, he said, exhausting its style and subject, "leaves behind it a burnt up field.")[20] Arcturus also suggests Stephen and major themes. In Greek myth Arcas (Arcturus), slain by his grandfather, is restored to life by his father, Zeus, who later prevents him from unwittingly killing his mother. Stephen, too, is a "slain" son resurrected, obsessed by but innocent of matricide. How much of this was Joyce's intention and how much is playing the game of "hunt the symbol" is certainly debatable, but at any rate there are the stars and there are the themes, and so long as the implications are treated as possibilities and not dogmatized into certainties they are worth considering.

700: The discoveries of Galileo, Marius, Piazzi, Le Verrier, Herschel and Galle may have been "independent," but hardly "synchronous," in the sense of contemporary, for their lives span four centuries, and commentators have been puzzled. Joyce may be ridiculing Bloom's ignorance, but more likely he is playing on "synchronous" to mean that the discoveries involved the synchronized movements of heavenly bodies. The "new moon with the old moon in her arms" is from the ballad of "Sir Patrick Spens." In the *Odyssey* (Book XIV), Ulysses predicts that he will return as the old moon wanes and the new appears. Eight years after Shakespeare's birth a nova did appear over delta in Cassiopeia, and another in Corona Septentrionalis in 1866, the year of Bloom's birth.

701: Babbling along at great rate about the appearance of various novae, Bloom finally runs down and peters out ludicrously with "and in and from other constellations some years before or after the birth or death of other persons."

702: The question listing the "special affinities...between the moon and woman" forms a little poem, a beautiful expression of an age-old theme. The following question, by contrast, is all the more ridiculous, with its mention of "paraffin oil lamp" and "Frank O'Hara, window blind, curtain pole and revolving shutter manufacturer, 16 Aungier street."

703: Commentators have had a heyday with the description of the meteor, and certainly the names involved are suggestive. "Vega" is the remnant of an Arabic phrase meaning "falling eagle," and together with "the

Lyre" (sometimes called "the Harp") suggests the Ireland from which Stephen is departing, Fall, Flight, and Poetry. Berenice was killed by her son. Richard Ellmann's more general comment here may point the safest path: "The sky...offers its distant configuration of a fusion taking place on earth."[21] With the opening of the gate we see that Bloom, his day as a "keyless citizen" at an end, now has a key.

704: The heighoing clock indicates half past the hour, or 2:30 a.m. Joyce's note for Stephen's "retreating feet" and the "jew's harp" reads, "SD bootsoles on flags of hollow lane twanged a fourfold chord." Bloom's "companions now in various manners in different places defunct" parallel the lost comrades of Ulysses.

705: The phrase "new solar disk" is a typescript substitution for the manuscript's "young sun," perhaps partly to avoid a too obvious pun on "son." "Limb" of the sun is used in its astronomical sense – the outer edge of a heavenly body. A minor controversy over Bloom's rearranged furniture provides a good illustration of the importance of being familiar with Joyce's rough notes. In a funny yet semi-serious article,[22] Hugh Kenner suggests that Molly, daunted by the actual appearance of eager Blazes Boylan, tried to evade or at least postpone "the physical moment" by getting him to move the furniture (pieces like the sideboard and piano, Kenner argues, would be too heavy for either or both Molly and Mrs. Fleming). So Boylan moved the furniture, but his inexhaustible sexuality was not dampened by his labors, and Molly was back at square one. Anyway, nice try on Molly's part. This interpretive excursion of Kenner's drew an indignant feminist rebuttal from Margaret Honton.[23] Molly or Mrs. Fleming certainly could have moved all the furniture, and all evidence points to Molly as eager for sex, and her nature as adventuresome, not evasive or hesitant. So there. All this makes engaging and amusing reading, and one hesitates to douse the fire. But if Kenner had seen, as we did in Chapter 2, Joyce's notes three times proclaiming that Molly (or MB), "will move furniture," he very likely would never have entertained his idea to begin with. And if Margaret Honton had seen the same notes, she could have handed Kenner his head.

706: Bloom's assumption that Mulligan is "Dr" Mulligan, made also in Circe (493) and Eumaeus (620), probably originated when Mulligan, first meeting Bloom in the maternity hospital, asked him if he was "in need of any professional assistance we could give" (403). Mulligan's amusing "gradation of green" is described on page 424.

707: The burning of incense is apparently a nightly ritual at 7 Eccles Street, for it was also burned the night before (63). On this night its main purpose is fumigation after Boylan, just as Ulysses, in the *Odyssey*, fumigates his rooms with sulphur. The clock, tree and owl, earlier called "matrimonial auguries" (694), are all wedding gifts and are stopped, frozen, artificial, dead, as is the Blooms' marriage. The clock stopped on the first day of spring, implying that for Bloom and Molly there will be no stirring of dull roots with spring rain. Significantly, the mantel clock in Bloom's dreamhouse will be a "guaranteed timekeeper" (713).

708: Nabokov admired the "wonderful catalogue" of Bloom's books, "clearly reflecting both his haphazard culture and his eager mind."[24] Many have turned up in his thoughts during the day, and they emphasize travel and science. *In the Track of the Sun* is listed here with "titlepage missing," although Bloom, thinking of this book in the previous morning, remembered, "Sunburst on the titlepage" (57); he may, of course, simply have been recalling a page once present but later lost, but more likely this is Joyce's slip. Joyce asked Frank Budgen to send him "Any bookseller's Catalogue, preferably old,"[25] from which he probably drew some of the bibliographical details here. The *Life of Napoleon* with "marginal annotations, minimising victories, aggrandising defeats of the protagonist" may have been suggested to Joyce by the titlepage of one of his own books: *"Life of Buonaparte, in Which the Atrocious Deeds, Which He Has Perpetrated, in order to Attain His Elevated Station, Are Faithfully Recorded; by Which Means Every Briton Will Be Enabled to Judge of the Disposition of His Threatening Foe; and Have a Faint Idea of the Desolation Which Awaits This Country, Should His Menaces Ever Be Realized."[26]

710: Joyce at one time considered a novel restitution of Bloom's lost trouser button: part of a note reads, "attach button by adhesive to back."

711: Calculating the time since a bee stung Bloom, Joyce again flunks a math test: it happened three, not two, weeks and three days ago. The note reads, "Is the bumblebee bite better?" Joyce, too, compiled budgets. Gorman reproduces a budget from Joyce's Paris notebook for a month in 1903.[27] Bloom is better off than his creator was then, for that budget ends, "Remainder — 0." Bloom's list of expenditures is not complete: omitted are the ten shillings he paid Bella Cohen (558) and the one shilling he also paid her for the broken lamp (585). Kenner suggests that these are omitted here because this budget is only "such a version as Bloom might let Molly inspect."[28] Perhaps so, but one wonders how Bloom might explain to Molly the budget's inclusion of that postal order (sent to Martha Clifford).

712: About boots, socks, and toenail. A note reads, "LB takes off boot...Ah!" During the ride to the cemetery in the Hades episode, Bloom thinks, "I wish Mrs Fleming had darned these socks better" (89); here, through his right sock his toenail has "again effracted." And another note is "LB's nail same smell as 20 yrs ago." Bloom's dreamhouse has probably attracted more attention than any other section of Ithaca. Adjectives like pathetic, grotesque, banal, consolatory appear among critical comments.

Of all the catalogues, here is the cornucopia of cornucopias, as Joyce follows his initial avalanche with the aftershocks of some twenty questions of elaborated expansion. The whole thing is infallibly sustained, infinitely touching, and increasingly funny. This long reverie of success and, later, failure is the conscious equivalent of the subconscious Circe hallucinations. Note here that like most husbands, Bloom allows Molly little place in his dreams (in Circe, she is "hastily removed in the Black Maria" [483]). After the description of Bloom's lavish bathroom, Molly's needs are summarily dismissed with "ditto, plain." And Molly might like to have "the whole place swimming in roses" (781), but there are no roses in Bloom's garden.

714: Don't miss that shaded sundial.

717: In the final proof Joyce changed "Irish Civil Service Building Society" to the text's present conglomerated travesty of all building societies. Among the books Joyce requested from Frank Budgen in November, 1921, was "any little manual on stamp collecting";[29] the passage on stamps here was added in galley proof during January, 1922.

718: No "government premium" for squaring the circle has ever existed. Bloom's scheme for a power plant "at head of water at Poula-phouca" had been carried out by the time Joyce wrote Ithaca.

719: An accidental ten-word omission following the list of railroads makes nonsense of the ending of this passage (see the list of misprints under "Errata" in Chapter 3).

720: The note for that "one sole unique advertisement" (typical Ithacan redundancy) is "Men stare at poster." Barely recovered from the dreamhouse flood, the reader now is buried in the detritus of that first table drawer. Kenner likens this to "an archaeologist's midden-hoard,"[30] and Marilyn French psychoanalyzes, "The usually locked drawer...is like the Circe chapter of the novel, full of the ludicrous and pathetic objects people feel it necessary to hide."[31]

721: Grover Smith, Jr., points out that Bloom's cryptogram, with its suppression of vowels, resembles traditional Hebrew, and "like certain Greek epigraphy, it is boustrophedonic (this term refers to the manner in which a field is plowed with oxen, in furrows started alternately at opposite boundaries). And the cipher quaintly echoes: 'OX...OKS.'"[32] Bloom's "erotic photocards" are no secret from Molly: "a nun maybe like the smutty photo he has shes as much a nun as Im not" (738). Many commentators have noted Bloom's ridiculous physical measurements, with an impossibly small chest and a calf larger than his thigh. Most have assumed satiric intentions on Joyce's part (R. M. Adams: "evidently deliberate and willful"[33]), but Kenner gets close to the truth when he suggests that Joyce probably used statistics printed as a testimonial letter in Eugen Sandow's *Strength and How to Obtain It.*[34] The testimonialist, Joyce failed to realize, was an exceptionally spindly specimen, and when Bloom's measurements were further reduced in the final text, impossibility resulted. If familiarity with Joyce's notes might have prevented Kenner from proposing that Boylan moved the furniture (see Glossary for p. 705), here is a case where the notes clinch his point. The following pairs of figures are before and after exercises:

Sandow testimonial		Joyce's notes	*Ulysses*
Chest	29, 32½	29, 32½	28, 29½
Biceps	10, 13	10, 13	9, 10
Forearm	9½, 12	9½, 12	8½, 9
Thigh	16½, 20	10½, 12	10, 12
Calf	11, 13	11, 13	11,12

With one exception, Joyce clearly copied exactly those testimonial figures into his notes. The exception is the "thigh," but we can easily imagine Joyce, working with less than keen concentration or eyesight, mistaking the testimonial "16½" for "10½" and losing his place and repeating the "12" from the preceding figure. Anyway, not realizing that the testimonial figures were skeletal to start with, Joyce assumed they were "normal," and with satiric intention after all proceeded to cut Bloom down even further in the book.

722: Zack Bowen points out the appropriateness of a Wonderworker testimonial from a soldier who, in Kipling's Boer War poem "The Absent-Minded Beggar," has "left a lot o' little things behind him."[35] Stephen earlier referred to Hamlet as "The absentminded beggar" (187).

723: Bloom's middle name probably comes from Paula Weiss, sister of Joyce's Zurich friend, Ottocaro Weiss.[36] Bloom's reminiscences of his father's senescence and death counterpoint his earlier memories of his daughter's birth, childhood, and adolescence.

724: The "tetragrammaton" is the four letters YHWH (Yahweh), ineffable because held too sacred to be profaned by utterance (cf. Bloom's cryptogram with "vowels suppressed" [721]).

725: The very comfort of Bloom's securities leads him to ponder possible "reverses of fortune."

726: Edmund Epstein reproves Stuart Gilbert for assuming that "latration" in the "latration of illegitimate unlicensed vagabond dogs" means "befouling," pointing out that Joyce coined the word from the Latin *latrare,* "to bark."[37] Nevertheless, it still suggests "befouling" by its association with the Latin *lavo, lavatrino* (Fr. *latrine*), and Joyce would hardly miss this. Bloom imagines himself pelted with "decomposed vegetable missiles, worth little or nothing or less than nothing"; in Circe, a mob hurls at him "objects of little or no commercial value," including "unsaleable cabbage" (492).

727: Don Juan O'Hara, with the English garrison at Gibraltar, took up bullfighting as an amateur in the 1870s and achieved remarkable success. The "bispherical moon" revealed through an "imperfectly occluded skirt" first arose in Bloom's mind in the Lotos Eaters episode: "Or their skirt behind, placket unhooked. Glimpses of the moon" (82 — and *Hamlet,* I:4:53).

728: Molly, who has already become a symbol of the earth ("You are mine. The world is mine." [662]), and the moon ("What special affinities appeared...to exist between the moon and woman?" [686]), now also becomes the sun, for Bloom will "somehow reluctantly, suncompelled, obey the summons of recall." The idea of recapitulating Bloom's activities in the form of Hebrew rites struck Joyce while he was revising the final proof, and he added the fifteen parentheses. It was additions like these, shattering the typography of an entire paragraph, that ultimately caused the French printers to parallel *merde* with a fine new swearword — JOYCE![38] Urim and Thummim were objects used by ancient Hebrews for divination by casting lots (see Exodus 28:30); Melchisedek, blessing Abraham, offered him bread and wine (Bloom's "unsubstantial lunch"); Simchath Torah ("Rejoicing in the Law") is the day on which the Torah, its cycle concluded, is read with special solemnity; Shira Shirim is simply "Song of Songs."

729: About that noisy table: a cancelled notesheet entry reads, "the table farted." The "selfinvolved enigma" of "Who was M'Intosh?" has produced involved attempts at identification. A favorite candidate is the character James Duffy in "A Painful Case." Since Joyce's brother Stanislaus has stated that *he* was the model for Duffy, the enigma deepens. According to Ellmann, Stuart Gilbert said M'Intosh is Wetherup, a friend of Joyce's father.[39] Joyce liked to bedevil his own friends by asking, "Who was the man in the mackintosh?" Perhaps the "lankylooking galoot" (109) was James Joyce. Anyway, by the time one has chased down all the mackintosh references in the novel and read the various critical theories, one no longer much gives a damn.

730: Bloom is "arrested" on entering the bedroom by Molly's resemblance to her father; Joyce's note is "MB has look of old Tweedy." The safety pin in Molly's drawers recalls the motif, "Mary lost the pin of her drawers" (78). Pin or not, Molly is little more able than Mary "To keep it up."

731: The Blooms' head-to-foot position in bed, besides symbolizing marital estrangement, suggests again the novel's theme of isolation and community. Like Bloom and Stephen in their "parallel course," Bloom and

Molly here are together but separate, aligned but opposed. To apply one of Bloom's earlier thoughts in a quite literal sense, "Both ends meet" (108).[40] Bloom's attitude toward the bed, especially now that Boylan has occupied it, is summed up in serpentine imagery: "snakespiral springs," "viper radii," "ambush of...adders." That list of Molly's "lovers" has caused trouble over the years. Early criticism tended to accept this passage as the horrible truth about promiscuous Molly, but later and more careful readers have rightly shown that the list is not nearly so damning as might appear. Its very wildness—ranging from bootblack, organgrinder, and farmer up through doctor, professor, priest, and lord mayor—is a warning. With most of the men, Molly has been adulterous only in passing fancy, not in fact. She herself, in her soliloquy, mentions several of them in terms of only slight acquaintance, and many of her "affairs" were merely mild flirtations or surprise encounters. Penrose saw her bathing before a window (754), Lenehan "had her bumping up against me" in a crowded carriage (234), the farmer at the horse show aroused her with his equestrian uniform (374), and the "unknown gentleman in the Gaiety Theatre" stared down at her from the dresscircle "with his operaglass for all he was worth" (284). Aside from Boylan, in fact, only one person in the list can be shown to have had any really amorous contact with Molly—Bartell d'Arcy (745)—and even that tryst is kept ambiguous. There is, however, a curious omission from the list. Where is Lieutenant Stanley Gardner, whom Molly mentions five times in Penelope in definitely erotic terms and to whom she gave Mulvey's ring (762)?

733: Bloom's "slaughter" of the suitors through an attitude of equanimity in which Molly's affair becomes as "natural as any and every natural act" recalls Simon Dedalus' "After all, it's the most natural thing in the world" (89) and prepares for Molly's "its only nature" (776) and "what else were we given all those desires for Id like to know" (777).

734: A notesheet entry about "families of curves" is puzzling: "family of curves (Pen) = slayer & slain." Penelope's curves are obvious enough, but the equation with "slayer & slain" is obscure. The note "Woman's arse honest" is probably the source for the text's description of female hemispheres as "insusceptible...of contrarieties of expression." Bloom's climactic arrival of Molly's promised land has been forecast by Bella Cohen's epithet, "Adorer of the adulterous rump!" (530) Herbert Howarth has suggested that Bloom's adoration is an image not only of pleasure and reconciliation, but also of guilt, prepared for by his confession in Circe, "I rererepugnosed in rerererepugnant" (538).[41]

735: Molly's "catechetical interrogation" parallels Penelope's in the *Odyssey* when she first meets Ulysses at his return, and Bloom's "modifications" in his replies parallel Ulysses' fabricated answers. It is easy to miss the full extent of Bloom's false account. To explain his long absence, "he included mention of a performance by Mrs Bandman Palmer of *Leah*"; that is, he tells Molly he attended this performance, which was followed by "an invitation to supper at Wynn's (Murphy's) Hotel." There has been, of course, no such invitation (the hotel is not even mentioned elsewhere in the book), and this much, at least, Molly understands: suspecting that Bloom has been in Nighttown, she soliloquizes, "and the hotel story he made up a pack of lies to hide it" (739). In manuscript Joyce also had Bloom mention "a charitable visit to the National Lying-In Hospital, 29, 30 and 31 Holles street," but cancelled this, true though it is, as incompatible with the *Leah* performance and supper invitation.

736: Only now does Joyce reveal that the Blooms have not had complete sexual intercourse for the past ten years, a fact bound to color in retrospect the reader's attitude to many of Bloom's thoughts during the day. Joyce does not say which of the two enforced this abstention, but a long finger points at Molly. The ten years began with baby Rudy's death ("that disheartened me altogether" [778]), and the present passage stresses female opposing male—the text's description of Bloom's "limitation of activity...in consequence of a preestablished natural comprehension in incomprehension between the consummated females (listener and issue)" is the Ithacan transformation of a blunt note: "Molly & Milly both turn on LB."

737: The description of Bloom and Molly "carried westward" by the "motion of the earth" seems at first to be simply an error in direction, until one realizes that careful Joyce realized that now, at about 3 a.m., the couple are swinging nocturnally "westward" toward the dawn which will initiate the diurnal "eastward" swing. For many years after *Ulysses* was published the general critical view of Molly, usually based on the description here of her lying "in the attitude of Gea-Tellus, fulfilled, recumbent, big with seed," was one of combined Mother Nature, Fertility Goddess, and Feminine Principle. Rebecca West, for example, described her as "the great mother who needs not trouble to trace her descent from the primeval age whence all things come, who lies in a bed yeasty with her warmth and her sweat."[42] In the late 1950s, however, two readers sharply challenged this view, and Molly has never since been quite the same. Molly's sleeping "in the attitude of Gea-Tellus," it was said, does not make her Gea-Tellus; she is averse to motherhood, to sexual relations with Bloom, to complete intercourse with Boylan.[43] More than this, she is a figure of "sterility, perversion, disease and death"; her soliloquy is "the bitterest and deadliest thing Joyce ever wrote": she is, in short, "the very center of paralysis."[44] Here again is the difficulty caused by the difference between Joyce's naturalistic surface and his symbolic subsurface—the difference noted earlier with the theme of isolation and community. A statement by Litz already quoted in Chapter 4 bears repeating here: "Any reading of *Ulysses* that aims at doing justice to Joyce's complex vision must be composed of constant adjustments and accommodations between myth and fact, and it is in 'Ithaca' that these adjustments are most difficult to make."[45] That Molly is presented mythically as "the great mother" just cannot be argued away; the evidence in the novel and in Joyce's notes and letters is incontrovertible. On the other hand, the naturalistic level of surface action presents evidence just as conclusive that she is, in "fact," far removed from the creative principle—sterile, perverted, indifferent (though hardly "the very center of paralysis"). J. I. M. Stewart observes that "there is a sense in which *Where?* receives its answer in Joyce's next book. Bloom has fallen asleep; we have accompanied him just over the threshold and thereby gained a preliminary glimpse of the vast territory of the unconscious mind into which we are to be conducted in *Finnegans Wake*. The jingle of names...is hypnoidal, and the strange resonance in *Darkinbad the Bright-dayler* expresses the violence done by the unconscious and its queer categories to the logic of waking life."[46] The closing words of Ithaca do anticipate the language of the *Wake,* but between that monolith and Ithaca lies Penelope, and it is Molly who provides the immediate answer to that ultimate *Where?* In her mind, in her psyche, Everyman Bloom is contained. He has traveled, he has obeyed the summons of recall, he now rests with her. Bloom's last thoughts, beginning with "Going to dark bed...," appear in Joyce's notes as "Very long time ago I was going to bed somewhere and there was a squareshaped or was it when I was where was that." This is precisely the unpunctuated, elliptical stream of Molly's consciousness, as subjective as Ithaca is objective. The questions of Ithaca have subsided into an unanswerable large black dot; Penelope provides the unquestionable Answer. All sorts of speculations have been made about that large black dot. It is the rok's egg, with Bloom inside, it is the circle Bloom hopes to square, it is the earth as seen from outer space, it is even Molly's anus. Might it not just be Leopold Bloom sound asleep? Ithaca's relentless interrogator has finally been silenced by a loud snore.

Appendix

The Rosenbach Manuscript

Since the Rosenbach manuscript of Ithaca marks the beginning of the process of accretion which continued through typescripts, galley proofs, and page proof, it is reproduced here for the reader's convenience. The following transcription, made directly from the manuscript itself, is as complete and accurate as multiple checking and collation could make it, including all details of spelling, punctuation, capitalization, and even careless slips of Joyce's pen.

In the transcription, each addition made directly to the basic text has been placed within single brackets. Double and triple brackets have been used to mark, respectively, an addition to an addition, and (rare absurdity) an addition to an addition to an addition. To avoid confusion with Joyce's text, bracketed *editorial* comments begin with the word "Note:" except for the many uses of "*sic,*" all of which are obviously editorial. For reasons that are obscure, Joyce placed red or green asterisks beside thirty-seven of the Manuscript questions. These questions here are immediately preceded by "[red star]" or "[green star]."

Ithaca

I

What course did Bloom and Stephen follow returning?

Lower and Middle Gardiner streets and Mountjoy square, west. Then, bearing left, (they) Gardiner's place by an inadvertence as far as the farther corner of Temple street. Then, bearing right, Temple street, north, as far as Hardwicke place. They crossed the circus before George's church diametrically, the chord in any circle being less than the arc which it subtends.

[*Note: Next five questions added on left-hand page of notebook*]

[Of what did they speak during their itinerary?

Music, literature, Ireland, Dublin, Paris, friendship, woman, diet, the influence of gaslight [[or the light of arc and glowlamps]] on the growth of [[adjoining]] trees, the Roman catholic church, Jesuit education, careers, the study of medicine, [[the past day]] Stephen's breakdown.

[Did Bloom discover similarity between their respective reactions to experience?

Both were sensitive to artistic impressions, musical in preference to plastic or pictorial. Both preferred [[a]] continental to [[an]] insular manner of life. Both indurated by early domestic training and an inherited tenacity of resistance professed their disbelief in [[many]] accepted religious, national, social and ethical doctrines. Both admitted the alternately stimulating and obtunding influence of heterosexual magnetism.

[Were their views on some points divergent?

Stephen dissented openly from Bloom's views on the importance of dietary and civic selfhelp while Bloom dissented tacitly from Stephen's views on the eternal affirmation of the spirit of man in literature. The collapse which Bloom ascribed to gastric inanition and certain chemical compounds of varying degrees of adulteration and alcoholic strength Stephen attributed to the reapparition of a matutinal cloud at first no bigger than a woman's hand.

[Was there one point were equal and negative? [*sic*]

The influence of gaslight or electric light on the growth of adjoining trees.

[Had Bloom discussed similar subjects during nocturnal perambulations in the past?

In 1884 with Owen Goldberg and Cecil Turnbull. In 1885 with Percy Apjohn. In 1886 (frequently) [[occasionally]] with casual acquaintances. In 1888 [[frequently]] with major

Brian Tweedy and his daughter Miss Marion Tweedy, together and separately. Once in 1892 and once in 1893 with Julius (Juda) Mastiansky.]

What action did Bloom make on their arrival at their destination?
At the housesteps of number 7 Eccles street he put his hand mechanically into the [*Note:* the *written over word* his] back pocket to get his latchkey.

Was it there?
It was in the corresponding pocket of the trousers which he had worn on the day but one preceding.

Why was he doubly irritated?
Because he had forgotten and because he remembered that he had reminded himself twice not to forget.

What were then the alternatives?
To enter or not to enter. To knock or not to knock.

His decision?
A stratagem. He climbed over the area railings, compressed his hat on his head, grasped the lower parts of two rails, lowered his body gradually by its length of five feet nine inches and a half to within two feet ten inches of the area pavement, and allowed his body to move freely in space, by separating himself from the railings and crouching in preparation for the impact of the fall.

Did he fall?
By his weight of ten stone and four ounces in avoirdupois measure, as certified by the graduated machine for periodical selfweighing in the premises of Francis Froedman, pharmaceutical chemist of 19 Frederick street, north, on the last feast of the Ascension, to wit, the twelfth day of May of the year one thousand nine hundred and four of the christian era.

Did he rise uninjured?
He rose uninjured though shocked by the impact, raised the latch of the area door by leverage, entered the kitchen through the scullery, ignited a lucifer match by friction, ̶h̶t̶ set free inflammable coal gas by turning on the ventcock, lit a high flame which, by regulating, he reduced to quiescent candescence and lit finally a portable candle.

Where was Stephen meanwhile?
Reclined against the area railings he perceived through the transparent kitchen panes a man regulating a gasflame, a man lighting a candle, a man removing in turn each of his two boots, a man leaving the kitchen holding a candle.

Did the man reappear elsewhere?
After a lapse of four minutes the glimmer of his candle was discernible through the glass fanlight over the halldoor. The halldoor turned gradually on its hinges. In the open space (thus) of the doorway the man reappeared without his hat, with his candle.

Did Stephen obey his sign?
Yes, entering softly, he helped to close and chain the door and followed softly along the

hallway the man's back and candle past a lighted crevice of doorway on the left and [carefully] down a turning staircase of more than five steps into the kitchen of Bloom's house.

What did Bloom do?

He extinguished the candle by a sharp injection of breath upon its flame, drew two [spoonseat deal] chairs to the hearthstone, [[one for Stephen with his back to the area window, the other for himself when necessary,]] [knelt on one knee,] composed in the grate a pyre of crosslaid resintipped sticks and various coloured papers and irregular polygons of [best] Abram coal [at twentyone shillings a ton] from the yard of Messrs Flower and M'Donald of 7 D'Olier street, kindled it at three projecting points of paper with one ignited wooden match.

Of what similar apparitions did Stephen think?

Of others elsewhere in other times who, kneeling on one knee or on two, had kindled fires for him, of Brother Michael in the infirmary of the college of the Society of Jesus at Clongowes Wood in the county of Kildare, of his father, Simon Dedalus, in the unfurnished room of his first residence in Dublin, number thirteen North Richmond [Fitzgibbon] street, of his godmother Miss Kate Morkan in the house of her dying sister Miss Julia Morkan at 15 Usher's Island, of his aunt Sara, wife of Richie (Richard Goulding) in the kitchen of their lodgings at 62 Clanbrassil street, of his mother in the kitchen of number twelve North Richmond street on the morning of the feast of Saint Francis Xavier 1898, of the dean of Studies, Father Butt, in the physics' theatre of university College, 16 Stephen's Green, north, of his sister Dilly (Delia) in his father's house in Cabra.

[What did Stephen see on raising his gaze to the height of a yard from the fire towards the opposite wall?

A curvilinear rope stretched between two holdfasts [[athwart]] across the recess beside the chimney pier from which hung four smallsized square handkerchiefs [[folded unattached consecutively in adjacent rectangles]] and one pair of grey Lisle ladies' stockings [[in their habitual position]] clamped by three erect wooden pegs two at their outer extremities and the third at their point of junction.]

(Of) What [*Note: capital* W *written over small* w] did Bloom think of their different ages? That neither could Stephen now have his age then nor he then Stephen's now.

By what act did he solve the problem?

He removed the saucepan to the left hob, rose and carried the iron kettle to the tap and sink in order to draw water by turning the cock [faucet] to let it flow.

Did it flow?

Yes. From Roundwood reservoir [in county Wicklow, capable of containing 2400 million gallons, through [[an aqueduct of]] filtered pipes mains by Callowhill to Stillorgan, a distance of 22 statute miles, and thence by an gradient of 250 feet to the city boundary at Leeson street bridge though] (near Stillorgan,) (where) from prolonged summer drouth the water had fallen below the sill of the overflow weir for which reason the borough surveyor on the instructions of the waterworks committee had prohibited the use of municipal water for purposes other than those of consumption particularly as the South Dublin Guardians notwithstanding their ration of 15 gallons per day per pauper supplied [through] a 6 inch meter had been convicted of a wastage of 20,000 gallons per night by a reading of their meter on the affirmation of the law agent of the corporation, Mr Ignatius Rice, thereby acting to the detriment of another section of the public, selfsupporting taxpayers, solvent, sound.

What in water did Bloom, carrying water, returning to the range, admire?
Its universality, its equality and constancy to its nature in seeking its own level, its vastness in the ocean of Mercator's projector, [its unplumbed profundity in the Sundam trench of the Pacific exceeding 8000 fathoms,] [[the restlessness of its waves and surface particles visiting in turn all points of its seaboard, its quiescence in calm, its turgidity in neap and spring tides, its preponderance of 3 to it [*sic*] over the dry land of the globe, its capacity to hold in solution all soluble substances including millions of tons of the most precious metals, its slow erosions of peninsulas and islands, its persistent formation of downwardtending promontories, its weight and volume and density, its gradation of colours in the torrid and temperate and frigid zones, its vehicular ramifications in continental lakecontained streams and [[[confluent]]] oceanflowing rivers [[[with their tributaries]]] and transoceanic currents, its violence in seaquakes and waterspouts, its vast circumterrestrial ahorizontal curve,]] its secrecy in springs exemplified by the well by the hole in the wall at Ashtown gate, [the simplicity of its composition, two parts of hydrogen with one of oxygen,] its healing virtues, [its buoyancy in the waters of the Dead Sea,] its properties for cleansing, quenching thirst and fire, nourishing plant life, its strength in rigid hydrants, its docility in working [hydraulic] millwheels, electric power stations, its utility in canals, rivers, if navigable, bleachworks, tanneries, scutchmills, its [submarine] fauna and flora, [numerically, the inhabitants of the globe, its ubiquity as it constituted 90% of the human body,] its noxiousness in marshes, faded flowers, pestilential fens, stagnant pools in the waning moon.

Having set the halffilled kettle on the now burning coals why did he return to the stillflowing tap?
To wash his soiled hands with a partially consumed tablet of lemonflavoured soap [to which paper still adhered] bought thirteen hours previously for threepence and still unpaid for in fresh cold neverchanging everchanging water and dry them, face and hands, in a long redbordered holland cloth passed over a wooden revolving roller.

What reason did Stephen give for declining Bloom's offer?
That he was hydrophobe, hating [total] contact ~~with~~ [by immersion in cold] water, his last bath having taken place in the month of October of the preceding year, disliking [the] acqueous substances of glass and crystal, distrusting aquacities of thought and language

What impeded Bloom from giving Stephen counsels of hygiene and prophylactic with suggestions concerning a preliminary wetting of the head [and contraction of the muscles with rapid splashing of the face and thoracic region] in case of sea or river bathing?
Aquacity.

What phenomenon took place in the vessel of liquid on the fire?
The phenomenon of ebullition. Convected heat was constantly and increasingly conveyed from the source of calorification to the liquid contained in the vessel, being radiated through the uneven unpolished dark surface of the metal iron, in part reflected, in part absorbed, in part transmitted, gradually raising the temperature of the water from normal to boiling point.

(How) What announced the accomplishment of this rise in temperature?
A [double] falciform ejection of water vapour from under the kettlelid at both sides simultaneously.

[For what personal purpose could Bloom have applied the water so boiled?
To shave himself.

[What advantages (accrued from) [[attended]] shaving by night?
A softer beard, quiet reflections upon the course of the day, a cleaner sensation when awaking after a fresher sleep since matutinal noises, premonitions and perturbations, a clattered milkcan, a postman's double knock, a shock, a shoot, with thought of aught he sought though fraught with nought might cause a faster rate of shaving and a nick, (for) [[on]] which incision plaster with precision, cut and humected and applied, adhered: which was to be done.]

What were the contents of the kitchen dresser when opened by Bloom?
On the lower shelf five vertical breakfast plates, six horizontal breakfast eups [saucers] on which rested inverted breakfast cups, a moustache cup, uninverted, and saucer of Crown Derby, four white goldrimmed eggcups, an open shammy purse displaying coins, mostly copper, a phial of aromatic comfits and a red bettingticket. On the middle shelf a chipped eggcup containing pepper, a drum of table salt, four black olives in oily paper, an empty (jar of) pot of Plumtree's potted meat, a Jersey pear, a halfempty bottle of William Gilbey and Co's white invalid port, a packet of Epps's soluble cocoa, [five ounces of Anne Lynch's choice tea at 2/- per lb in a crinkled leadpaper bag] a bowl [a cylindrical canister containing the best crystallised] (of) lump sugar, a bisected onion [two onions, one bisected, the larger, Spanish, entire, the other, smaller, Irish, bisected and more redolent], a jar of Irish Model dairy's cream, a jug [containing a naggin and a quarter of] (of) soured milk [which added to the quantity subtracted for Mr Bloom's and Mrs Fleming's breakfasts, made one pint, the total quantity originally delivered], two cloves, a halfpenny and a small dish containing a slice of fresh ribsteak. On the upper shelf a battery of jamjars (empty) of various sizes.

How did Bloom prepare a meal [collation]?
He poured into two teacups two [level] spoonfuls, four in all, of Epp's soluble cocoa.and proceeded according to the directions for use printed on the label. [*Note: the clear presence in the manuscript of a period after "cocoa" indicates that the following twelve words are an addition; if so, however, they were added at the time Joyce was writing the basic text, for he provided space for them before beginning the next question.*]

What marks of special hospitality did the host show his guest?
Relinquishing his right to the moustache cup of imitation crown Derby presented to him by his only daughter, Millicent he drank from a cup identical with that of his guest and served to his guest and, in reduced measure, to himself the cream usually reserved for his the breakfast of his wife Marion (Molly)

Was the guest conscious of [and did he acknowledge] these attentions [marks of hospitality]?
His attention was directed to them by his host jocosely, and he accepted them (in silence) seriously [as they drank in silence].

Who drank more quickly?
Bloom, having the advantage of (a few) [ten] seconds at the start and and [*sic*] taking three sips to his opponent's one.

What cerebration accompanied his act?
Concluding that his silent companion was engaged in mental composition he reflected on

the pleasures derived from literature of instruction rather than of amusement as he himself had applied to the works of Shakespeare more than once for the solution of difficult problems in imaginary or real life.

Had he found their solution?
In spite of careful and repeated reading of certain passges, aided by a glossary, he had not derived conviction from the text.

What lines concluded his first piece of original verse written at the age of 11 in 1877 (written) on the occasion of [the offering of] three prizes of 10/-, 5/- and 2/6 respectively (offered) for competition by the Shamrock [, a] weekly newspaper?

> *An ambition to Squint*
> *At my verses in print*
> *Makes me hope that for these you'll find room.*
> *If you so condescend*
> *Then please place at the end*
> *The name of yours truly, L. Bloom*

Did he find four separating forces between his temporary guest and him?
Name, age, race, creed.

What anagrams had he made on his name in youth?
Leopold Bloom
Ellpodbomool
Molldopeloob
Bollopedoom
Old Ollebo, M.P.

What acrostic upon the abbreviation of his first name had he sent to Miss Marion (Molly) *Tweedy on the 14 February 1888*? [*Note: underlining hastily, Joyce mistook the last line of the question for the first line of the answer.*]

> *Poets oft have sung in rhyme*
> *Of music sweet their praise divine.*
> *Let them hymn it nine times nine.*
> *Dearer far than song or wine.*
> *You are mine. The world is mine.*

What relation existed between their ages?
16 years before [in] 1888 when Bloom was of Stephen's present age Stephen was 6. Sixteen years after in 1920 when Stephen would be of Bloom's present age (Bloud) Bloom would be 54.

What events might nullify these calculations?
The cessation of existence of both or either, the inauguration of a new era or calendar, the annihilation of the world.

Had Bloom and Stephen met before that day?
Twice. The first time in the lilacgarden of Matthew Dillon's house, Medina Villa, Kimmage

road, Roundtown, in 1887, [in the company of his mother,] Stephen being then of the age of 5 and reluctant to give his hand in salutation. The second time in the coffeeroom of Breslin's hotel [on a rainy Sunday in the January] in [of] 1892, [in the company of his father and his granduncle,] Stephen being then 5 years older.

Did Bloom accept the invitation to dinner given by the son and afterwards seconded by the father?
Very gratefully, appreciatively, sincerely, regretfully, he declined.

Did their conversation on the subject of these reminiscences reveal a third connecting link between them?
Mrs Riordan (Dante), a widow of independent means, had resided in the house of Stephen's parents from 1 September 1888 to 29 December 1891 and had also resided from during the years 1892, 1893 and 1894 in the City Arms Hotel owned by Elizabeth O'Dowd of 54 Prussia street where during parts of the years 1893 and 1894, she had been a constant informant of Bloom who resided also in the same hotel, being at that time a clerk in the employment of Joseph Cuffe of 5 Smithfield for the superintendence of sales in the [adjacent] Dublin Cattle market of the North Circular road.

Had he performed any special corporal work of mercy for her?
He had sometimes wheeled [propelled] her [on warm summer evenings], an infirm widow of independent, if limited, means, in her bathchair with (some) slow revolutions of its wheels as far as the corner of the North Circular road opposite Mr Gavin Low's place of business where she had remained for a certain time scanning through his onelensed fieldglasses unrecognisable citizens on tramcars, roadster bicycles, hackney carriages, tandems, private and hired landaus, dogcarts, ponytraps and brakes passing from the city to the Phoenix Park and *vice versa.*

Why could he support [that] (t)his vigil with the greater equanimity?
Because in middle youth he had often sat observing through a [glass] boss of a multicoloured pane the spectacle offered with continual changes of the thoroughfare without, pedestrians, quadrupeds, velocipedes, vehicles, passing slowly, quickly, evenly, round and round and round the rim of a round precipitous globe.

[What distinct different memories had each of her now eight years deceased?
The older, her bizique cards and counters, her Skye terrier, her supposititious wealth, her lapses of responsiveness: the younger, her lamp of colza oil before the statue of the Immaculate Conception, her green and maroon brushes for Parnell and for Michael Davitt, her tissue papers.]

Were there no means still remaining to him to achieve the rejuvenation which these reminiscences divulged to a younger companion rendered the more desirable?
The indoor exercises, formerly intermittently practised, subsequently abandoned, prescribed in Eugene Sandow's *Physical Strength and How to Obtain It* which, designed particularly for commercial men engaged in sedentary occupations, were to be made with mental concentration in front of a mirror so as to bring into play the various families of muscles and produce successively a pleasant rigidity, a more pleasant relaxation and the most pleasant repristination of juvenile agility.

Had any special agility been his in earlier youth?

Though ringweight lifting had been beyond his strength and the full circle gyration beyond his courage yet as a high school scholar he had excelled in his stable and protracted execution of the half lever movement on the parallel bars in consequence of his abnormally developed abdominal muscles.

See II p. 1

[*Note: here Joyce shifted to the second notebook, labeled "Ithaca II."*]

Did either openly allude to their racial difference?
Neither.

What did Bloom think that Stephen thought about Bloom?
He thought that he thought that he was a jew whereas he knew that he knew that he knew that he was not.

What were their respective parentages?
Bloom, only male heir of Rudolf Virag (subsequently Rudolph Bloom) of Szombathely, Milan, London and Dublin and of Margaret [Higgins] second daughter of Julius Higgins (born Karoly) and Fanny Higgins (born Hegarty). Stephen, eldest [surviving] male heir of Simon Dedalus of Cork and Dublin and of Mary, daughter of Richard and Christina Goulding (born Grier).

Had Bloom and Stephen been baptised?
(Stephen on) Bloom three times, by the reverend Mr Gilmer Johnston M.A. [alone] [[in the [[[protestant]]] church of Saint Nicholas Without, Coombe]], by James O'Connor, Philip Gilligan and James Fitzpatrick [together, under a pump in the village of Swords], and by the reverend Charles Malone, C. C., in the church of the Three Patrons, Rathgar. Stephen (once) by the reverend Charles Malone, C. C. [alone] in the church of the Three Patrons, Rathgar.

~~Were~~ [Did they find] their educational careers similar?
Bloom had passed successively through a dame's school and the high school: Stephen through the preparatory, junior, middle and senior grades of the intermediate and through the matriculation, first arts, second arts and degree courses of the university.

Why did Bloom refrain from stating that he had frequented the university of life?
Because of his incertitude as to whether ~~Stephen had said this to him already or he himself had said it to Stephen.~~ [this observation had or had not been already made by him to Stephen or by Stephen to him.]

What two temperaments did they individually represent?
The scientific. The artistic.

What proofs did Bloom (give) [adduce] to prove that his tendency was towards applied, rather than to pure, science?
Certain [possible] inventions of which he had cogitated when reclining on his back in a state of repletion to aid digestion, stimulated by his appreciation of the importance of inventions now common but once revolutionary, for example, the parachute, the corkscrew, the safety pin, the canal lock.

Were these inventions principally intended for an improved scheme of kindergarten?

Yes. They comprised astronomical kaleidoscopes exhibiting the twelve constellations of the zodiac from ~~the~~ Aries to Pisces, arithmetical gelatine lozenges, geometrical to correspond to zoological biscuits, globemap playing balls, historically costumed dolls.

What ~~encouraged~~ [also stimulated] him in his cogitations?

The financial success achieved by Ephraim Marks and Charles A. James, the former by his ~~penny~~ [1d] bazaar at 42 George's street, south, the latter at 6½ d shop and world's [fancy] fair [and] waxwork exhibition at 30 Henry Street, admission ~~sixpence~~ [6d], children 1d: and the infinite possibilities hitherto unexploited of the modern art of advertisement if condensed in triliteral symbols of magnetised efficacy? ["?" *sic*]

Such as?

K. 11. Kino's 11/- Trousers.

House of Keyés. Alexander J. Keyes.

Such as not?

Look at this long candle. Calculate when it burns out and you receive gratis 1 pair of our special non-compo boots boots [*sic*], guaranteed 1 Candle power. Address: Barclay and Cook, 18 Talbot street.

What is home without Plumtree's Potted Meat?

Incomplete.

With it an abode of bliss.

Manufactured by George Plumtree, 23 Merchant's quay, Dublin [put up in 4 oz. pots], and inserted by Councillor J. [Joseph] P. Nannetti, M. P., Rotunda Ward, 19 Hardwicke street, under the obituary notices and anniversaries of deceases. The name on the ~~jar~~ [label] is Plumtree. [A plumtree in a meatpot, registered trade mark.]

Which example did he adduce to induce Stephen to comprehend that originality does not invariably conduce to success?

His own ideated and rejected project of an illuminated showcart, drawn by a beast of burden, in which two smartly dressed girls were to be seated engaged in writing.

What [suggested] scene ~~did this suggest to~~ [was then constructed by] Stephen?

A solitary hotel in mountain pass. Autumn. Twilight. A fire lit. In dark corner a young man seated. A young woman enters. Restless. She sits. She goes to the window. She stands. She sits. Twilight. She thinks. On solitary hotel paper she writes. She thinks. She writes. She sighs. Wheels and hoofs. She hurries out. He comes from his dark corner. He seizes the solitary paper. He holds it towards the fire. Twilight. He reads.

What?

In sloping, upright and backhands: Queen's Hotel, Queen's Hotel, Queen's Hotel, Queen's Ho...

What [suggested] scene ~~did this suggest to~~ [was then reconstructed by] Bloom?

The Queen's Hotel, Ennis, county Clare where Rudolph Bloom (Rudolf Virag) died on the 27 June 1886 of an overdose of ~~acenite~~ monkhood (aconite) in the form of a neuralgic liniment composed of 2 parts of aconite liniment to 1 of chloroform liniment

Did he attribute this homonymity to [information or] coincidence or intuition?
Coincidence.

[Did he depict the scene in words [[verbally]] for his guest [[to see]]
He preferred himself to see and listen to another's words by which potential narration was
realised and kinetic temperament relieved.]

Did he see only a [second] coincidence in the second scene narrated to him, described by the
narrator as *A Pisgah Sight of Palestine* or *The Parable of the Plums*?
It, with the preceding scene and with others unnarrated by [but] existent by implication,
seemed to him to contain in itself [and in conjunction with the personal equation] certain
possibilities of financial [,social, personal and sexual] success, whether contributed in printed
form [, following the precedent of Philip Beaufoy or Doctor Dick or Heblon's *Studies in
Blue,*] to a publication of certified circulation and solvency or employed verbally as
intellectual stimulation for (a) sympathetic auditors during the increasingly long nights gradually following the summer solstice.

Which domestic problem as much as, if not more than, any other frequently engaged his
mind?
What to do with our wives.

What had been his hypothetical [singular] solutions?
Parlour games (dominos, bezique, halma, tiddledywinks, draughts, or chess or back-
gammon): embroidery, darning or knitting for the policeaided clothing society: musical duets,
mandoline and guitar, piano and flute, guitar and piano: legal scrivenery or envelope address-
ing; courses-of-even biweekly visits to variety entertainments: commercial activity in a cool
dairy shop or warm cigar divan: the clandestine satisfaction of erotic irritation in masculine
brothels, state-inspected and medically controlled: courses of evening instruction specially
designed to render instruction agreeable.

What instances of deficient mental development [in his wife] inclined him in favour of the
(lastmentioned) eighth solution?
In disoccupied moments she had more than once covered a sheet of paper with signs and
hieroglyphics which she stated were Greek and Irish characters. She had interrogated constantly at [varying] intervals as to the correct method of writing the capital initial of the name
of a city in Canada, Quebec. She understood little of political complications, internal or
external. In calculating the addenda of bills she frequently had recourse to digital aid.
Unusual (words) polysyllables of foreign origin she interpreted phonetically or by false analogy or by both: metempsychosis (met him pike hoses), *alias* (a mendacious person mentioned
in scripture).

How had he attempted to remedy this state of comparative ignorance?
Variously. By leaving in a conspicuous place a certain book open at a certain page, by
assuming in her when alluding explanatorily (a) [latent] knowledge, by open ridicule in her
presence of some absent other's ignorant lapse. (By direct instruction.)

With what success? [had he attempted direction instruction?]
She followed not all, a part of the whole, gave attention with interest, comprehended with
surprise, with care repeated, with greater difficulty remembered, forgot with ease, with
misgiving remembered, repeated with error.

[What system had proved more effective?
Indirect suggestion implicating selfinterest.

[Example?

4   3

She disliked umbrella with rain, he liked woman with umbrella, she disliked rain with
1   2
new ·hat, [[he liked woman with new hat,]] he bought new hat with rain. She carried
umbrella with new hat.]

Accepting the analogy implied in his guest's parable which examples of postexilic ~~greatness~~
[eminence] did he adduce?
Three seekers of the pure truth, Moses of Egypt, Moses Maimonides, author of More
Nebukim (Guide of the Perplexed) and Moses Mendelssohn of such eminence that from
Moses (of Egypt) to Moses (Mendelssohn) there arose none like Moses (Maimonides).

[What statement was made, under correction, by Bloom concerning a fourth seeker of pure
truth, by name Aristotle, mentioned by Stephen?
That the seeker mentioned had been a pupil of a rabbinical philosopher, name uncertain.]

What fragments of verse from the ancient Hebrew and ancient Irish languages were cited
[with modulations of voice and translation of texts] by guest to host and by host to guest?
By Stephen: *suil, suil, suil arun, suil go siocair agus suil go cuin* (walk, walk, walk your
way, walk in safety, walk with care).
By Bloom: *Kifeloch harimon rakatejch m'baad l'zamatejch* (thy temple amid thy hair is as a
slice of pomegranate).

How was a glyphic comparison of the phonic symbols of both languages? [*sic*]
[By juxtaposition.] On the penultimate blank page of a book entitled *Sweets of Sin* (produced by Bloom [and so manipulated that its front cover came in contact with the surface of
the table)] with a pencil (supplied by Stephen) Stephen wrote the Irish characters for gee, eh,
dee, em, simple and modified, and Bloom in turn wrote the Hebrew characters ~~goph~~ ghimel,
aleph, daleth and (in the absence of mem) a substituted goph, explaining their arithmetical
values of 3, 1, 4, and 100.

[Was the knowledge possessed by both of each of these languages, the extinct and the
revived, theoretical or practical?
Theoretical, being confined to some rules of grammar and syntax and practically excluding
vocabulary.

[What points of contact existed between these languages and the peoples who spoke them?
The presence of guttural sounds in both [[languages]], their antiquity ~~of both~~, both having
taught [*sic*] on the plain of Shinar 242 years after the deluge in the seminary instituted by
Fenius Farsaigh, descendant of Noah, progenitor of Israel, and ascendant of Heber and
Heremon, progenitors of Ireland, their vast [[archeological]] genealogical and historical and
religious literatures comprising the works of rabbis and culdees, Torah, Talmud, Pentateuch,
Book of the Dun Cow, Book of Ballymote, Book of Kells: their dispersal, persecution, survival and revival: the restoration in Chanah David of Zion and the possibility of Irish
political autonomy or devolution.

[What anthem did Bloom chant partially in anticipation of that consummation?
Kolod balejwaw pnimah
Nefesch, jehudi, homijah.

[Why did he not conclude?
In consequence of defective mnemotechnic.

[How did he compensate for this deficiency?
By a periphrastic version of the general text.]

In what common study did their mutual reflections merge?
The increasing simplification traceable from the Egyptian hieroglyphs to the Greek and Roman alphabets and the anticipation of modern stenography [and telegraphic code] in the cuneiform inscriptions (Semitic) and the virgular ogham writing (Celtic).

Did the guest comply with his host's request?
Doubly, by appending his signature in Irish and Roman characters.

      was
What ~~were~~ Stephen's auditive (~~and visual~~) sensation*s*?
He heard in a profound ancient male unfamiliar melody the accumulation of the past,~~-the predestination-of-the-future~~.

What was Bloom's visual sensation?
He saw in a quick young male familiar form the predestination of a future.

What [future] careers had been possible for him in the past and with what exemplars?
In the church, Roman, Anglican or Nonconformist: exemplars, the very reverend John Conmee S. J., the reverend T. Salmon, D D, provost of Trinity college, Dr. Alexander J. Dowie. At the bar [, English or Irish,]: exemplar, Seymour Bushe, K. C., Rufus Isaacs, K. C. On the stage, modern or Shakespearean: exemplars, Charles Wyndham, high comedian, Osmond Tearle (†1901), exponent of Shakespeare.

Did the host encourage his guest to chant in a modulated voice a strange legend on an allied theme?
Reassuringly, their place [where none could hear them talk,] being secluded, reassured, the prepared beverages having been consumed.

Recite [the first (major) part of] this chanted legend?

> *Little Harry Hughes and his schoolfellows all*
> *Went out for to play ball.*
> *And the very first ball little Harry Hughes played*
> *He drove it o'er the jew's garden wall.*
> *And the very second ball little Harry Hughes played*
> *He broke the jew's windows all.*

How did the host receive this first part?
Smiling, a jew, he heard with pleasure and saw the unbroken kitchen window.

Recite the second part (minor) of the legend.

> *Then out came the ~~old~~ jew's daughter*
> *And she all dressed in green.*
> *"Come back, come back, you pretty little boy,*
> *And play your ball again"*
>
> *"I can't come back and I won't come back*
> *Without my schoolfellows all.*
> *For if my master he did hear*
> *He's make it a sorry ball"*
>
> *She took him by the lilywhite hand*
> *And led him along the hall*
> *Until she led him to a room*
> *Where none could hear him call.*
>
> *She took a penknife out of her pocket*
> *And cut off his little head*
> *And now he'll play his ball no more*
> *For he lies among the dead.*

How did the host receive this second part?
Unsmiling, he heard and saw with wonder a jew's daughter, Millicent (Milly), all dressed in green.

Condense Stephen's commentary.
One of all, the least of all, is the victim predestined. Once by inadvertence, twice by design he challenges his destiny. It comes when he is abandoned and challenges him reluctant and, as an apparition of hope and youth, holds him unresisting. It leads him to a strange habitation, to a secret infidel apartment, and there, implacable, immolates him, consenting.

Why was the host silent?
He weighed the possible evidences for and against ritual murder: the incitations of the hierarchy, the superstition of the populace, the ~~desire of persecution~~ [envy of opulence:] the influence of retaliation, the sporadic reappearance of atavistic delinquency, the mitigating circumstances of fanaticism, hypnotic suggestion and somnambulism.

See I p. 9

[*Note: here Joyce shifted back to the first notebook.*]

Had this [latter or any cognate] phenomenon declared itself in any member of his family?
Twice, in Holles street and in Ontario terrace, his daughter Millicent (Milly) at the ages of 6 and 8 years had ~~exclaimed~~ uttered in sleep an exclamation of terror and had replied to the interrogations of two figures in night attire with a vacant mute expression

What other infantile memories had he of her?
15 June 1889. A querulous female infant crying to cause and lessen ~~pain~~ [congestion]. A

child renamed Padney Socks she shook with shocks her moneybox: counted his three free buttons one, tloo, tlee: a doll, a boy, a sailor she threw away: ~~fair~~ [blond], born of two dark, she had blond ancestry, remote, a [~~military~~] violation, Herr Hauptmann Hainau, ~~a soldier~~ [Austrian army,] proximate, a hallucination, lieutenant Mulvey, British navy

What endemic characteristics were present?
Conversely the nasal and frontal formation was derived in a direct line of lineage which, though interrupted, would continue at distant intervals to its most distant intervals.

What memories had he of her adolescence?
She relegated her skippingrope to a recess. On the duke's lawn entreated by an English visitor, she declined to permit him to make and take away her photographic image. On the South Circular road in the company of Elsa Potter, followed by an individual of sinister aspect, she went half way down Stamer street and turned abruptly back. On the vigil of the 15th anniversary of her birth she wrote a letter from Mullingar, county Westmeath, making a brief allusion to a [local] student.

Did that first division, portending a second division, afflict him?
Less than he had imagined, more than he had hoped.

What second departure was contemporaneously perceived by him ~~and~~ differently, if similarly?

(margin numbers: 3   2   1)

A temporary departure of his cat.

Why similarly, why differently?
Similarly, because actuated by a secret purpose, the quest of a male or of a healing herb. Differently, because of different possible returns to the inhabitants or to the habitation.

In other respects were their differences similar?
In passivity, in economy, in the instinct of tradition, in unexpectedness.

As?
Leaning she sustained her blond hair for him to ribbon it for her. On the free surface of the lake in Stephen's green amid inverted reflections of trees her uncommented spit, describing concentric circles of waterrings, indicated by the constancy of its permanence the locus of a somnolent prostrate fish. In order to remember the date, combatants, issue and consequences of a famous military engagement she pulled a plait of her hair. Silly Milly, she dreamed of having had an unspoken unremembered conversation with a horse whose name had been Joseph to whom (which) she had offered a tumblerful of lemonade which it (he) had appeared to have accepted.

[*Note: in the margin opposite the last sentence above, Joyce wrote "ecrivez les paroles en parenthesis"*]

(margin numbers: 2   1)

In what way had he utilised given gifts as matrimonial auguries to interest and to instruct her?
As object lessons to explain: 1) the nature and habits of oviparous animals, the possibility of aerial flight, certain abnormalities of vision, the secular process of imbalsamation: 2) the principle of the pendulum, exemplified in bob, wheelgear and regulator, the translation in terms of human or social regulation of the various positions of moveable indicators on an

unmoving dial, the exactitude of the recurrence per hour of an instant in each hour, when the longer and the shorter indicator were at the same angle of inclination, *videlicet,* $5^5/_{11}$ minutes past each hour per hour in arithmetical progression.

In what manners did she reciprocate?
She remembered: on the 27th anniversary of his birth she presented to him a breakfast moustachecup of imitation crown Derby porcelain ware. She provided: at quarter day or thereabouts if or when purchases had been made by him not for her she showed herself attentive to his necessities, anticipating his desires. She admired: a natural phenomenon having been explained by him to her she expressed the immediate desire to possess without [gradual] acquisition a fraction of his science, [the moiety], the quarter, a thousandth part.

What proposal did Bloom, diambulist, father of Milly, somnambulist, make to Stephen, noctambulist?
To pass in repose the hours intervening between Thursday (proper) and Friday (normal) on an extemporised cubicle in the apartment immediately above the kitchen and immediately adjacent to the sleeping apartment of his host and hostess.

What various advantages would or might have resulted from a prolongation of such an extemporisation?
For the guest: security of domicile and seclusion of study. For the host: rejuvenation of intelligence, vicarious satisfaction. For the hostess: disintegration of obsession, acquisition of correct Italian pronunciation.

Was the proposal accepted?
Promptly, inexplicably, with amicability, gratefully it was declined.

What counterproposals were alternately advanced, accepted, modified, declined, restated in other terms, reaccepted, ratified, reconfirmed?
To inaugurate a series [course] of Italian instruction, place the residence of the instructed. To inaugurate a course of vocal instruction, place the residence of the instructress. To inaugurate a series of static, semistatic and peripatetic intellectual dialogues, places the residence of both speakers (if both speakers were resident in the same place), the *Ship* hotel and tavern, 6 Lower Abbey street (W. and E Connery, proprietors), the National Library of Ireland, 10 Kildare street, the National Maternity Hospital, 29, 30 and 31 Holles street, a public garden, the vicinity of a place of worship, a conjunction of two or more streets public thoroughfares, the point of bisection of a right line drawn between their residences (if both speakers were resident in different places).

What rendered problematic [for Bloom] the realisation of these mutually selfexcluding proposals [propositions]?
The irreparability of the past: once at a performance of Albert Hengler's circus in the Rotunda, Rutland square, Dublin an intuitive [particoloured] clown [in quest of paternity] had penetrated from the ring to a place in the auditorium where Bloom, solitary, was seated and had publicly declared to an exhilarated audience that he (Bloom) was his (the clown's) papa. The imprevidibility of the future: once in [the summer of] 1898 he (Bloom) had marked a florin (2/-) with three notches on the milled edge and tendered it in payment of an account due to and received by J and T Davy, family grocers, 1 Charlemont Mall, Grand Canal, for circulation on the waters of civic finance, for possible, circuitous or direct, return.

Was the clown Bloom's son?
No.

Had Bloom's coin returned?
Never.

Why would a recurrent frustration the more depress him?
Because at the critical turningpoint of human existence he desired to amend many social conditions, the product of inequality and avarice and international animosity.

He believed then that human life was infinitely perfectible, eliminating these conditions?
There remained the generic conditions imposed by natural, as distinct from human law: the necessity of destruction to procure alimentary sustenance, the painful character of birth and death, the monotonous menstruation of simian and (particularly) human females extending from the age of puberty to the menopause, ~~catastrophic~~ inevitable accidents at sea, in mines and factories, certain very painful maladies and their resultant surgical operations, innate lunacy and criminality, catastrophic cataclysms which make terror the basis of human mentality, seismic upheavals the epicentres of which are located in densely populated regions, the fact of vital growth from infancy through maturity to decay.

Why did he desist from speculation?
Because it was a task for a ~~high~~ superior intelligence to substitute other phenomena in place of those to be removed.

Did Stephen participate in his dejection?
He affirmed his significance as a conscious rational reagent between a micro and a macrocosm constructed upon the incertitude of the void.

Was this affirmation apprehended by Bloom?
Not literally, substantially.

What spectacle confronted them when they, first the host, then the guest, emerged [silently, doubly dark,] by a passage from the rere of the house into the garden?
The heaventree of ~~the~~ stars hung with humid nightblue fruit.

With what meditations did Bloom accompany his demonstration to his companion of various constellations?
Meditations increasingly vaster: of the infinite lattiginous scintillating uncondensed milky way, of Sirius 9 lightyears distant and in volume 900 times the dimension of our planet, of Arcturus, of Orion with belt and nebula in which 100 of our solar systems could be contained, of moribund, of nascent new stars such as Nova in 1901, of our system plunging towards the constellation of Hercules, of the parallax or parallactic drift of socalled fixed stars, in reality evermoving wanderers from immeasurably remote eons to infinitely remote futures in comparison with which the years, threescore and ten, of allotted human life formed a period of infinitesimal brevity.

Why did he not elaborate these calculations to a more precise result?
Because ~~he had learned~~ some years previously in 1886 when occupied with the problem of the quadrature of the circle he had learned of the existence of a number [computed to be] of such magnitude, e.g., the 9th power of the 9th power of 9, that 33 closely printed volumes of

1,000 pages each of innumerable quires and reams of India paper would have to be requisitioned in order to contain the complete tale of its printed integers.

Did he find the problem of the inhabitability of the ~~stars~~ [planets] and their satellites easier of solution?

Of a different order of difficulty. Conscious that the human organism when elevated to a considerable altitude in the terrestrial atmosphere suffered from nasal hemorrhage, impeded respiration and vertigo, when proposing this problem for solution, he had conjectured that ~~an~~ a more ancient and differently constructed race of beings might subsist otherwise under Martian, Mercurial, Veneral, Jovian, Saturnian, Neptunian or Uranian conditions, though humanity would probably there as here remain inalterably attached to vanities of vanities.

His logical conclusion?

The it was a Utopia, a past which possibly ~~no longer~~ had ceased to exist before its spectators had entered existence.

Was he more convinced of the esthetic value of the spectacle?

Indubitably in consequence of the reiterated examples of poets in the delirium of ~~love~~ the frenzy of love or in the abasement of rejection invoking resplendent constellations or the frigidity of the satellite of their planet? ["?" *sic*]

Did he then accept the theory of astrological influences?

It seemed to him as possible of proof as of confutation and the nomenclature employed in its ~~geographi~~ semelographical [*sic*] charts as attributable to verifiable intuition as to (erroneous) fallacious analogy: the lake of dreams, the seas of rains, the gulf of dews, the ocean of fecundity.

What special affinities appeared to him to exist between the moon and woman?

Her antiquity in preceding and surviving successive generations, her nocturnal predominance, her satellitic dependence, her luminary reflection, her constancy under all her phases, rising and setting by her appointed times, waxing and waning, the invariability of her aspect, her potency over effluent and refluent waters, the tranquil inscrutability of her visage, her omens of tempest and of calm, the stimulation of her light, her motion and her presence, the admonition of her craters, her arid seas, her silence: her splendour, when visible, her attraction, when invisible.

What visible luminous sign attracted Bloom's, who attracted Stephen's, gaze?

[In the second story (rere) of his (Bloom's) house] The light of a paraffin oil lamp with oblique shade projected on a screen of roller blind supplied by Frank O'Hara, window blind, curtain pole and revolving manufacturer, [*sic*] 16 Aungier street.

How did he elucidate the mystery of an invisible person, his wife Marion (Molly) Bloom, indicated by a visible vigilant luminous sign, a lamp?

With indirect and direct verbal allusions or affirmations: with subdued affection and admiration: with description: with impediment: with suggestion.

Both then were silent?

Silent, each contemplating the other in both mirrors of the flesh of fellowfaces.

Were they indefinitely inactive?

At Stephen's suggestion, at Bloom's instigation both, first Stephen, then Bloom, in penumbra urinated, their sides contiguous, their organs of micturition reciprocally rendered invisible by manual circumposition, their gazes, first Bloom's, then Stephen's, elevated to the projected luminous and semiluminous shadow.

Similarly?

The trajectories of their, first sequent, then simultaneous, urinations were dissimilar: Bloom's longer, less irruent, [in the[[incomplete]] form of the] bifurcated ante penultimate letter who in his ultimate year at High School (1880) had been capable of attaining the point of greatest altitude against the whole strength of the institution 210 scholars: Stephen's higher, more sibilant, who in the ultimate hours of the previous day had augmented by consumption an insistent vesical pressure.

What different problems presented themselves to each concerning the invisible audible organ of the other?

To Bloom: the problems of irritability, tumescence, rigidity, reactivity, dimension, sanitariness, pelosity. To Stephen: the problem of the sacerdotal integrity of Jesus circumcised (1 January, holiday of obligation to hear mass and abstain from unnecessary servile work) and the problem as to whether the divine prepuce, the carnal bridal ring of the [holy] Roman catholic apostolic church, conserved in Calcata, were deserving of simply hyperduly or of the fourth degree of latria accorded to the abscission of divine hair and toenails.

[Alone, what did Bloom hear?
The double reverberation of retreating feet, the double twang of a jew's harp in the resonant lane]

Alone, what did Bloom feel?
The cold of interstellar space, thousands of degrees below zero of Fahrenheit, Centigrade or Réaumur: the incipient intimations of proximate dawn.

What prospect of what phenomenon inclined him to remain?
The disparition of three final stars, the diffusion of daybreak, the apparition of a new young sun.

Had he ever been a spectator of that phenomenon?
Once, in 1887, after a [protracted] performance of charades in the house of Luke Doyle, Kimmage he had awaited with patience the apparition of the diurnal phenomenon, seated on a wall, his gaze turned in the direction of the east.

He remembered the initial paraphenomena?
More active air, a matutinal distant cock, ecclesiastical clocks at various points, avine music, the isolated tread of an early wayfarer, the visible diffusion of the light of an invisible luminous body, the first golden limb of the resurgent sun perceptible low on the horizon.

See II, p. 8

[*Note: here Joyce shifted again to the second notebook.*]

What suddenly arrested his (progress) ingress?
His right temporal lobe came into contact with a solid timber angle where, an infinitesimal

but sensible fraction of a second later, a painful sensation was located in consequence of antecedent sensations transmitted and registered.

Describe the alterations effected in the disposition of the articles of furniture?

A sofa upholstered in prune plush had been translocated from opposite the door to the ingleside near the compactly furled Union Jack (an alteration which he had frequently intended to execute), the blue and white checker inlaid majolicatopped table had been placed opposite the door in the place vacated by the prune plush sofa: the walnut sideboard (a projecting angle of which had arrested his ingress) had been moved from its position beside the door to a [more advantageous but more perilous] position in front of the door: two chairs had been moved from right and left of the ingleside to the position originally occupied by the blue and white checker inlaid majolicatopped table.

[Green star]
Describe them.

One: a squat stuffed easychair [, with stout arms extended and back slanted to the rere,] which ~~pushed~~ repelled in recoil had upturned an irregular fringe of a rectangular rug and displayed on its amply upholstered seat a centralised diffusing and diminishing discolouration. The other: a slender splayfoot [chair] of glossy cane curves, placed directly opposite the former, its frame from top to ~~middle~~ [seat] and from ~~middle~~ [seat] to base being varnished dark brown, its ~~middle~~ [seat] being a bright circle of white (woven) plaited rush.

[What significances attached to these two chairs?
Significances of similitude, of posture, of symbolism, of circumstantial evidence, of testimonial supermanence.]

What occupied the position originally occupied by the sideboard?

A vertical piano (Cadby) with exposed keyboard, its closed coffin supporting a pair of long yellow ladies' gloves and an emerald ashtray containing four consumed matches, a partly consumed cigarette and two discoloured ends of cigarettes, its musicrest supporting the music [in the key of G natural for voice and piano] of *Love's Old Sweet Song* (words by G. Clifton Bingham, composed by J. L. Molloy, sung by Madame Antoinete Sterling) open at the last page with the final indications ad libitum, forte, pedal, animato, sustained pedal, ritirando, close.

[Green star]
With what sensations did Bloom contemplate in rotation these objects?

With strain, elevating a candlestick: with pain feeling on his right temple a [contused] tumescence: with attention, focusing his gaze on a large dull passive and slender bright active: with amusement, remembering Dr Malachi Mulligan's scheme of colour containing the gradation of green: with pleasure, repeating the words and antecedent act and perceiving through various channels of internal sensibility the consequent and concomitant tepid pleasant diffusion of gradual discolouration.

His next proceeding?

From an open box on the majolicatopped table he extracted a black diminutive cone, 1 inch in height, placed it on its circular base on a small tin plate, placed his candlestick on the right corner of the mantelpiece, produced from his waistcoat a folded typed letter, unfolded the folded letter, examined it superficially, rolled it into a thin cylinder, ignited it in the candleflame, applied it when ignited to the apex of the cone till the latter reached the stage of rutilance, placed the cylinder in the basin of the candlestick disposing its unconsumed part in such a manner as to facilitate total combustion.

What followed?
That crater summit of the diminutive volcano emitted a vertical and serpentine fume redolent of aromatic oriental incense.

[Green star]
What objects, other than the candlestick, stood on the mantelpiece?
A timepiece of striated marble, stopped at the hour of 4.46 a.m. on the 21 March 1896, matrimonial gift of Matthew Dillon, a dwarf tree of glacial arborescence under a [transparent] bellshade, matrimonial gift of Luke and Caroline Doyle: an embalmed owl, matrimonial gift of Alderman John Hooper.

[Green star]
What interchanges of looks took place between these three objects and Bloom?
In the mirror of the giltbordered pierglass the undecorated back of the dwarf tree regarded the upright back of the embalmed owl. Before the mirror the matrimonial gift of Alderman John Hooper with a clear melancholy wise bright motionless compassionate gaze regarded Bloom while Bloom with obscure tranquil profound motionless compassionated gaze regarded the matrimonial gift of Luke and Caroline Doyle.

What composite image in the mirror then attracted his attention?
The image of a solitary [mutable] man.

Why solitary?
Brothers and sisters had he none.
Yet that man's father was his grandfather's son.

Why mutable?
From infancy to maturity he had ressembled [sic] his maternal procreatrix. From maturity to senility he would increasingly resemble his paternal procreator.

What final visual impression was communicated to him by the mirror?
The [optical] reflection of several inverted ~~books~~ volumes [with scintillating titles] on the two bookshelves opposite.

Catalogue these books.
Thom's Dublin Post Office Directory 1886
Dennis Florence M'Carthy's Poetical Works
Shakespeare's Works (dark crimson morocco, goldtooled)
The Useful Ready Reckoner (brown cloth)
The Secret History of the Court of Charles II (red cloth)
The Child's Guide (blue cloth)
The Beauties of Killarney (wrappers)
When We Were Boys by William O'Brien M. P. (green cloth, slightly faded)
Thoughts from Spinoza (maroon leather)
Philosophy of the Talmud (sewn pamphlet)

Lockart's Life of Napoleon (cover wanting, marginal annotations, minimising victories, aggrandising defeats of the protagonist)

Soll und Haben (black boards)

A Handbook of Astronomy (cover, brown leather, detached, 5 plates, antique letterpress long primer, author's footnotes pica, marginal clues brevier)

The Hidden Life of Christ (black boards)

In the Track of the Sun (yellow cloth, titlepage missing)

Physical Strength and How to Obtain It by Eugene Sandow (red cloth)

Short but yet Plain Elements of Geometry written in French by F. Ignat.

Pardies and rendered into English by John Harris D. D., London, printed for R. Knaplock at the Bishop's Head, MDCCXI, with dedicatory epistle to his worthy friend Charles Cox, esquire, Member of Parliament for the burgh of Southwark and having ink calligraphed statement on the flyleaf certifying that the book was the property of Michael Gallagher, dated this 10th day of May 1822, and requesting the finder, if the book should be lost or go astray, to restore it to Michael Gallagher, carpenter, Dufery Gate, Ennisicorthy, county Wicklow, the finest place in the world.

[Green star]
What reflections occupied his mind during the process of reversion of the inverted volumes?

The necessity of order, a place for everything and everything in its place: the deficient appreciation of literature possessed by females: the incongruity of an apple incuneated in a tumbler and of an umbrella inclined in a closestool: the insecurity of hiding any secret document behind, beneath or between the pages of a book.

Why, firstly and secondly, did he not consult the work in question?

Firstly, in order to exercise mnemotechnic: secondly, because after an interval of amnesia, when [, seated at the central table,] about to consult the work in question, he remembered by mnemotechnic the name of the military engagement, Plevna.

What iff caused him irritation in his sitting posture?

Inhibitory pressure of collar (size 17) and waistcoat (5 buttons), two articles of clothing superfluous in the costume of mature males and inelastic to alterations of mass by expansion.

[Green star]
How was the irritation allayed?

He removed his collar, with contained black necktie and collapsible stud, from his neck to a position on the left of the table. He unbuttoned successively [in reversed direction] waistcoat, trousers, shirt and vest along the medial line of irregular incrispated black hairs extending in triangular convergence from the pelvic basin over the circumference of the abdomen and umbilicular fossicle along the medial line of nodes to the intersection of the sixth pectoral vertebra, thence produced both ways at right angles and terminating in circles described about two equidistant points, right and left, on the summits of the mammary prominences.

What involuntary actions followed?

He compressed between 2 fingers the flesh circumjacent to a cicatrice [in the left infracostal region below the diaphragm] resulting from a sting inflicted 2 weeks and 3 days previously (23 May 1904) by a bee. He scratched [imprecisely] with his right hand, though insensible of prurition, various points and surfaces of his partly exposed wholly abluted skin. He inserted his left hand into the left lower pocket of his waistcoat and extracted and replaced a-shill a silver coin (1 shilling), placed there (presumably) on the occasion [(10 October 1903)] of the interment of Mrs Emily Sinico, Sydney Parade.

Did the process of divestiture continue?
Sensible of a benignant persistent ache in his footsoles he extended his foot to one side and observed the creases, protuberances and salient points caused by foot pressure in the course of walking repeatedly in several different directions, then, inclined, he disnoded the laceknots, unhooked and loosened the laces, took off each of his two boots for the second time, detached the partially moistened right sock through the fore part of which the nail of his great toe had again effracted, raised his right foot and, having unhooked a purple elastic
2   1
sock suspender, took off his right sock, placed his right unclothed foot on the ledge margin of the seat of his chair, picked at and gently lacerated the protruding part of the great toenail, raised the part lacerated to his nostrils and inhaled the odour of the quick, then, with satisfaction, threw away the lacerated unghial [*sic*] fragment.

Why with satisfaction?
Because the odour inhaled corresponded to other odours inhaled of other unghial fragments, picked and lacerated by Master Bloom, pupil of Mrs Jowett's juvenile school, patiently each night in the act of [brief] genuflection and nocturnal prayer and ambitious meditation.

In what ultimate ambition had all concurrent and consecutive ambitions now coalesced?
[Not to inherit or possess in perpetuity] an extensive demesne of 100 [a sufficient number of acres,] roods and perches, [surrounding a] baronial hall with gatelodge and carriage drive nor, on the other hand, a terracehouse or semidetached villa, described as *Rus in Urbe* or *Qui si sana,* but to purchase by private treaty in fee simple a thatched [bungalowshaped] dwellinghouse of southerly aspect, [with porch covered by parasitic plants (ivy or Virginia creeper), rising, if possible, upon a gentle eminence and standing in 5 or 6 acres of its own ground,] situate at a given point not less than 1 statute mile from the periphery of the metropolis, [within a time limit of not more than 15 minutes from tram or train line,] (e.g., Dundrum, south, or Sutton, north, both [localities] equally reported by trial to resemble the terrestrial poles in being miles and standing in 5 or 6 acres of its own ground [favourable climates for phthisical subjects),] the premises to be held under feefarmgrant, lease 999 years, the messuage to consist of 1 drawingroom, 1 sittingroom, 4 bedrooms, bathroom (hot and cold), tiled kitchen with close range and scullery, lounge hall fitted with linen wallpresses, dinner gong and comfortable corner fitments, [and pyramidically prismatic central chandelier lustre,] water closet with tipup seat, outoffices, coal and wood cellarage with winebin for distinguished guests, if entertained, gas throughout.

[What facilities of transit were desirable?
When citybound frequent connection by train or tram from their respective intermediate station or terminal. When countrybound velocipedes, a chainless freewheel roadster cycle with side basketcar attached, or drought conveyance, a donkey with wicker trap or smart phaeton with good working cob.]

What additional attractions might the grounds contain?
As addenda, a tennis and fives court, a glass summerhouse with tropical palms, equipped

in the best botanical manner, a rockery with waterspray, an orchard, kitchen garden and a vinery, all protected ~~from~~ [against] illegal trespassers by glasstopped mural enclosures.

What improvements might be subsequently introduced?
A rabbitray and fowlrun, a sundial shaded and sheltered by laburnum or lilac trees, a harmonically accorded Japanese tinkle gatebell, a capacious waterbutt, a lawnsprinkler with hydraulic hose.

[Green star]
What might be the name of this residence?
Bloom Cottage. Saint Leopold's. Flowerville.

[Green star]
Could Bloom of 7 Eccles street foresee Bloom of Flowerville?
In loose allwool garments with Harris tweed cap, price 8/6, and garden boots and wateringcan, trundling a weedladen wheelbarrow without excessive fatigue at sunset amid the scent of newmown hay.

[What mental ~~recreations~~ [[occupations]] were simultaneously possible?
Snapshot photography, comparative study of religions, folklore relative to various amatory and superstitious practices, contemplation of the celestial constellations.

[What lighter recreations?
House carpentry with a toolbox containing hammer, awl, nails, screws, tintacks, gimlet, tweezers, bullnose plane and turnscrew.]

Might he become a gentleman farmer?
Not impossibly, with 1 or 2 stripper cows, 1 pike of upland hay and requisite farming implements, e.g., an end-to-end churn, a turnip pulper etc.

What would be his social status among the county families and landed gentry?
Successively, that of gardener, groundsman, cultivator, breeder, and at the zenith of his career, resident magistrate or justice of the peace with a family crest and coat of arms and appropriate classical motto.

[Green star]
What course of action did he outline for himself in such capacity?
A course that lay between undue clemency and excessive rigour, the dispensation of unbiassed justice, tempered with mitigants but exactable to the uttermost farthing. Loyal to the core with an innate love of rectitude his aims would be the strict maintenance of public order, the repression of many abuses though not of all simultaneously, the upholding of the letter of the law (common, statute and law merchant) against all instigators of international persecution, all perpetuators of international animosities, all violators of domestic connubiality.

Prove that he had loved rectitude from his earliest youth.
To master Percy Apjohn at High School in 1880 he had divulged his disbeliefs in the tenets of the Irish (protestant) church [(to which his father Rudolph Virag) (later Rudolph Bloom) had been converted from the Israelitic faith and communion in 1865 by the Society for

promoting Christianity among the jews)] subsequently abjured by him in favour of Roman catholicism at the epoch of [and with a view to] his ~~marriage~~ [matrimony] in 1888 in favour of Roman catholicism. [*sic*] To Daniel Magrane [and Francis Wade] in 1882 during a juvenile friendship (terminated by the premature emigration of the former) he had advocated during nocturnal perambulations the evolutionary theories of Charles Darwin, expounded in *The Descent of Man* and *The Origin of Species*. In 1885 he had publicly expressed his adherence to [the collective [[and national]] economic programme advocated by James Fintan Lalor, John Fisher Murray, John Mitchel, J. F. X. O'Brien and others,] the agrarian policy of Michael Davitt, the constitutional agitation of ~~the William-Ewart Gladstone (later the~~ Charles Stewart Parnell (M. P. for Cork City), the programme of peace, retrenchment and reform of William Ewart Gladstone (M. P. for Midlothian) and, in support of his [political] convictions, had climbed up into a secure position ~~on a~~ amid the ramifications of a tree on Northumberland road to see the entrance into the capital of a demonstrative torchlight procession in escort of Viscount Ripon and (honest) John Morley.

> practically
> ~~Was his ambition realisable?~~
> ~~Yes~~

How much and how did he propose to pay for this country residence?

As per prospectus of the Irish Civil Service Building Society (incorporated 1874), a maximum of £ 60 per annum, being ⅙ of an assured income, representing at 5% simple interest a capital of £1200 of which ⅓ to be paid [~~by the society to the~~] on acquisition and the balance in the form of rent, viz, £800 plus 2½% interest on the same, repayable [quarterly] in equal annual rates until extinction of loan advanced for purchase within a period of 20 years, amounting to an annual rental of £64, headrent included, the titledeeds to remain in possession of the lender or lenders with a saving clause envisaging forced sale, foreclosure and mutual compensation in the event of protracted failure to pay the terms assigned otherwise the messuage to become the absolute property of the tenant occupier upon expiry of the period of years stipulated.

What rapid but insecure means to opulence might facilitate immediate purchase?

A private wireless telegraph which would transmit by dot and dash system the result of a national won by an outsider at odds of 50 to 1 at 3 hr 8 m p m at Ascot (Greenwich time) the message being received and available for betting purposes [in Dublin] at 2.59 p. m. (Dunsink time). A prepared scheme [based on a study of the laws of probability] to break the bank at Monte Carlo. A solution of the secular problem of the quadrature of the circle, premium £1,000,000 sterling.

Was vast wealth acquirable through industrial channels?

The reclamation of [dunams of] waste [arenary] soil, proposed in the prospectus of Agendath Netaim, Bleibtreustrasse, Berlin, W. 15, by the cultivation of orange plantations and melonfields [and reafforestation.] The utilisation of waste paper, fells of sewer rodents, human excrement possessing chemical properties, in the view of the vast production of the first, vast number of the second and immense quantity of the third, every normal human being of average vitality and appetite producing annually a sum total of 3 cwt to be multiplied by 4,235,000 the total propulation of Ireland according to the census returns of 1901.

Were there schemes of wider scope?

A scheme to be formulated and submitted for approval to the harbour commissioners for the exploitation of white coal, (hydraulic power), obtained at Dublin bar or Poulaphouca or Powerscourt for the economic production of electricity. A scheme to enclose the peninsular delta of the North Bull at Dollymount and transform it from a [erect on the space of the foreland] [[used for]] golf links and rifle ranges, casinos, booths, shooting galleries, hotels, boardinghouses, readingrooms, establishments for mixed bathing. A scheme for the use of dogvans and goatvans for the delivery of early morning milk. A scheme for the repristination of passenger and goods traffics over Irish waterways, when freed from weedbeds. A scheme to connect by tramline the Cattle Market (North Circular road and Prussia street) with the quays (Sheriff street, lower and East Wall), the cost of [acquired rolling stock for animal transport and of] additional mileage operated by the Dublin United Tramways Company, limited, to be covered by graziers' fees.

[Green star]
Was it possible to contract for these several schemes?
Given the support [, by deed of gift during donor's lifetime or by bequest after donor's painless extinction,] of eminent financiers (Blum Pasha, Rothschild, Guggenheim, Hirsch, Montefiore, Morgan, Rockefeller) possessing fortunes in 6 figures [, amassed during a successful life,] and joining capital with opportunity the thing required was done.

[Green star]
For what reason did he meditate on schemes so difficult of realisation?
It was one of his axioms that similar meditations or the automatic relation to himself of a narrative concerning himself or tranquil recollection of the past when practised habitually before retiring for the night alleviated fatigue and produced as a result sound repose and renovated vitality.

His justifications?
As a physicist he had learned that our of the 70 years of complete human life at least 2/7, viz, 20 years are passed in sleep. As a philosopher he knew that at the termination of any allotted life only an infinitesimal part of any person's desires has been realised. As a physiologist he believed in the artificial placation of malignant agencies chiefly operative during somnolence.

What did he fear?
The committal of homicide or suicide during sleep by an aberration of the light of reason, the incommensurable categorical intelligence situated in the cerebral convolutions.

What were habitually his final meditations?
Of some one sole unique advertisement to cause passers to stop in wonder, a poster novelty, with all extraneous accretions excluded, reduced to its simplest and most efficient terms not exceeding the span of casual vision and possessing the velocity of modern life.

See I p. 17

[*Note: here Joyce shifted back to the first notebook.*]

What did the first drawer unlocked contain?
A Vere Foster's handwriting copybook, [property of Milly (Millicent) Bloom,] certain pages of which bore diagram drawings marked *Papli,* which showed a large globular head with 5 hairs erect, 2 eyes in profile, the trunk full front with 3 large buttons, 1 triangular foot:

2 fading photographs of queen Alexandra of England and of Maud Branscombe, actress and beauty: a Yuletide card, bearing on it a pictorial representation of a parasitic plant, the legend *Mizpah,* the date Xmas 1892, the name of the senders: from Mr and Mrs M. Comerford, the versicle: *May this Yuletide bring to thee, Joy and peace and welcome glee*: a butt of red partly liquified sealing wax, obtained from the stores department of Messrs Hely's, Ltd, 89, 90, and 91 Dame street: an old sandglass which rolled containing sand which rolled: a sealed prophecy [(never unsealed)] written by Leopold Bloom in 1886 concerning the consequences of the passing into law of William Ewart Gladstone's Home Rule bill of 1886 (never passed into law): a bazaar ticket No 2004, of S. Kevin's Charity Fair, price 6d, 100 prizes: a cameo brooch, property of Ellen Bloom (born Higgins), [deceased]: a cameo scarfpin, property of Rudolph Bloom (born Virag), deceased: 3 typewritten letters, addressee, Henry Flower, c/o P. O. Westland Row, addresser, Martha Clifford, c/o P. O. Dolphin's Barn: the name and address of the addresser of the 3 letters in reversed alphabetic cipher, Nzigsz Xorunliw Wloksrmh Yzim: a press cutting from an English weekly periodical *Modern Society,* subject the corporal chastisement in girls' schools: a pink ribbon which had festooned an Easter egg in the year 1899: two partly uncoiled rubber preservatives with reserve pockets, purchased by post from Box 320, P. O. Charing Cross, London, W. C.: 1 pack of 1 dozen creamlaid envelopes, now reduced by 3: some assorted Austrian-Hungarian coins: 2 coupons of the Royal and Privileged Hungarian Lottery: a lowpower magnifying glass: 2 erotic photocards showing a) buccal coition between [nude] senorita and nude torero b) anal violation [by male religious (fully clothed)] of female religious (partly clothed), purchased by post from Box 320, P. O., Charing Cross, London, W. C.: a press cutting of recipe for renovation of
o l d
hats tan boots; a 1d stamp, lavender, of the reign of Queen Victoria: a chart of measurements of Leopold Bloom compiled before, during and after 2 months of consecutive use of Sandow-Whiteley's pulley exerciser, men's 15/–, athlete's 20/–, viz., chest 28 in and 29 ½ in, biceps 9 in and 10 in, forearm 8½ and 9 in, thigh 10 in and 12 in, calf 11 in and 12 in: 1 prospectus of the Wonderworker, the world's greatest remedy for rectal complaints, direct from Wonderworker, Coventry House, South Place, London E. C., addressed (erroneously) to Mrs L. Bloom with brief accompanying note commencing (erroneously): Dear Madam.

[Red star]
~~What advantages did the prospectus claim for this remedy?~~
[Quote the textual terms in which the prospectus claimed notable advantages for this remedy.]
It heals and soothes while you sleep, in case of trouble in breaking wind, assists nature in the most formidable way, insuring instant relief in discharge of gases, keeping parts clean and free natural action, an initial outlay of 7/6 making a new man of you and life worth living. Ladies find Wonderworker especially useful, a pleasant surprise when they note delightful result like a cool drink of fresh spring water on a sulty summer's day. Recommend it to your lady and gentlemen friends, lasts a lifetime. Insert long round end. Wonderworker.

[Red star]
Were there testimonials?
Numerous. From clergyman, British naval officer, wellknown author, city man, hospital nurse, lady, mother of five, absentminded beggar.

How did absentminded beggar's testimonial conclude?
What a pity the government did not supply our men with wonderworkers during the South African campaign! What a relief it would have been!

What object did Bloom add to this collection of objects?
a [3rd 4th] typewritten letter received by Henry Flower from Martha Clifford.

Why pleasant reflection accompanied this action?
The reflection that, apart from the letter in question, his face, form and address had been favourably received during the course of the preceding day by a wife (Mrs Josephine Breen, born Josie Powell), a nurse, Miss Callan (Christian name unknown), a maid, Gertrude (Gerty, family name unknown).

[Red star]
What possibility suggested itself?
The possibility of executing exercising virile power of fascination in the not immediate future after an elegant expensive repast in a private apartment in the company of an elegant courtesan, of corporal beauty, moderately mercenary, variously instructed, a lady by origin.

What did the 2nd drawer contain?
Documents: the birth certificate of Leopold Paula Bloom: an endowment policy [of £100] in the Scottish Widow's Assurance Society intestated Millicent (Milly) Bloom, payable at 21 years: a bank passbook issued by the Ulster Bank, College Green branch, showing a statement of a/c for halfyear ending 31 December 1903, balance in depositor's favour: £ 18-14-6 [(eighteen pounds, fourteen shillings and sixpence, sterling)], net personalty: dockets of the Catholic Cemeteries' [(Glasnevin)] Committee, relative to a graveplot purchased: a [local] press cutting concerning change of name by deedpoll.

Quote the textual terms of this notice.
I, Rudolph Virag, now resident at no 52 Clanbrassil street, Dublin, formerly of Szombathely in the kingdom of Hungary, hereby give that I have assumed and intend henceforth upon all occasions and at all times to be known by the name of Rudolph Bloom.

What other objects relative to Rudolph Bloom (born Virag) were in the 2nd drawer?
An indistinct daguerreotype of Rudolph Virag and his father Leopold Virag executed in the year 1852 in the portrait atelier of their (respectively) 1st and 2nd cousin, Stefan Virag of Szesfehervar, Hungary. An letter ancient hagadah book in which a pair of hornrimmed convex spectacles inserted marked the passage of thanksgiving in the ritual prayers for Pessach (Passover): a photocard of the Queen's Hotel, Ennis, proprietor, Rudolph Bloom: an envelope addressed *To my Dear Son Leopold.*

What reminiscences did these objects evoke in Bloom?
An old man widower, unkempt of hair, in bed, with head covered, sighing: an infirm dog, Athos: veronal resorted to by [increasing doses of] grains and scruples as a palliative of recrudescent neuralgia: the face in death of a suicide by poison.

Why did Bloom experience a sentiment of remorse?
Because in immature impatience he had treated with disrespect certain paternal beliefs and practices.

As?
The prohibition of the use of fleshmeat and milk at one meal: the circumcision of male infants: the supernatural character of Judaic scripture: the sanctity of the sabbath.

How did these beliefs and practices now appear to him?
Not more rational than they had then appeared, not less rational than other beliefs and practices now appeared.

What first reminiscence had he of Rudolph Bloom (deceased)?
Rudolph Bloom (deceased) narrated to his son Leopold Bloom [(aged 6)] a retrospective arrangement of migrations and settlements in and between Dublin, London, Florence, Milan, Szombathely, with statements of satisfaction (his grandfather having seen Maria Theresia, empress of Austria, queen of Hungary), with commercial advice (having taken care of pence, the pounds having taken care of themselves). Leopold Bloom [(aged 6)] had accompanied this narrations [sic] by constant consultation of a geographical map of Europe (political) and by suggestions for the establishment of affiliated business premises in the various centres mentioned.

Had time equally but differently obliterated the memory of these migrations in narrator and listener?
In narrator by the access of years and in consequence of the use of narcotic toxin: in listener by the access of years and in consequence of the action of distraction upon vicarious experiences.

What idiosyncracies of the narrator were concomitant products of amnesia?
Occasionally he ate ~~with hatted~~ without having previously removed his hat. Occasionally he drank voraciously the juice of gooseberry fool from an inclined plate. Occasionally he removed from his lips the traces of food by means of a lacerated envelope or other fragment of paper.

What two phenomena were more frequent?
The myopic digital calculation of coins, eructation consequent upon repletion.

What object offered partial consolation for these reminiscences?
The endowment policy, the bank passbook, the certificate of the possession of scrip.

[Red star]
From what reverse of fortune did these supports protect their possessor?
Mendicancy: that of the sandwichman, distributor of throwaways, nocturnal vagrant, maimed sailor, blind stripling, bailiff's man. Poverty: that of the outdoor ~~commerce~~ hawker of imitation jewellery, [sic] the dun for the recovery of bad and doubtful debts, the poor rate and deputy cess collector.

[red star]
With which attendant indignities?
The ~~contempt~~ [indifference] of previously amiable females, the contempt of males, the ~~receipt~~ acceptance of fragments of bread, the simulated ignorance of casual acquaintances, the latration of illegitimate vagabond dogs, the infantile discharge of vegetable missiles.

By what could such a situation be precluded?
By decease: by departure.

Which preferably?
The latter.

What considerations rendered it not entirely undesirable?
Constant cohabitation impeding mutual toleration of personal defects. The habit of independent purchase increasingly cultivated.

What considerations rendered it not irrational?
The parties concerned [, uniting,] had increased and multiplied, which being done, ~~and~~ offspring produced and educed to maturity, the parties, if ~~still united~~ [not disunited] for increase and multiplication were obliged to reunite to form the original couple of [uniting] parties, which was absurd.

What considerations rendered it desirable?
The attractive character of certain localities in Ireland and abroad.

~~As?~~ In Ireland?
~~In Ireland~~. The cliffs of Moher, the windy wilds of Connemara, lough Neagh with submerged petrified city, the Giant's Causeway, Fort Camden and Fort Carlisle, the Golden Vale of Tipperary, the islands of Aran, the pastures of royal Meath, Brigid's elm in Kildare, the Queen's Island shipyard in Belfast, the Salmon Leap, the lakes of Killarney.

Abroad?
Ceylon, [(with spice gardens supplying tea to Tom Kernan)] the temple of Jerusalem (where meeting was convened from year to year), the straits of Gibraltar (the unique birthplace of Marion Tweedy), the Parthenon (containing statues of nude ~~Greek~~ Grecian divinities), the Wall street money market (which controlled international finance), the Plaza de Toros at La Linea, Spain (where O'Hara of the Camerons had slain the bull), Niagara (over which no human being had passed with impunity), the land of the Eskimos (eaters of soap), the forbidden country of Thibet (from which no traveller returns), the bay of Naples (to see which was to die), the dead sea.

[Red star]
What public advertisement would divulge the occultation of the departed?
£5 reward, missing gent about 40, height 5 ft 8½ inches, full build, olive complexion, may have since grown a beard, when last seen was wearing a black suit. Above sum will be paid for information leading to his discovery.

[Red star]   no   no
Would the departed never ~~anywhere somehow~~ reappear?
Ever he would wander to the extreme limit of his cometary orbit, beyond the fixed stars and variable suns and telescopic planets, astronomical waifs and strays, passing from land to land, among peoples, amid events. Somewhere imperceptibly he would hear and obey the summons of recall. Disappearing from the constellation of the Northern Crown he would somehow reappear reborn above delta in the constellation of Cassiopeia and after incalculable eons of peregrination return an avenger, a wreaker of justice on malefactors, a dark crusader, a sleeper awakened, with financial resources surpassing those of Rothschild or of the silver king.

[Red star]
What rendered departure undesirable and irrational?
The lateness of the hour, the obscurity of the night, the uncertainty of thoroughfares, the

necessity for repose, the proximity of a [n occupied] bed, the anticipation of warmth (human) tempered with coolness (linen).

What advantages were possessed by an occupied, as distinct from an unoccupied bed?
The removal of nocturnal solitude, the stimulation of matutinal contact, the economy of mangling done on the premises in the case of trousers accurately folded and placed lengthwise between the spring mattress and the woollen mattress.

What [past] consecutive causes of fatigue did Bloom, before rising, silently enumerate?
The preparation of breakfast, the bath, the funeral, the advertisement of Alexander Keyes, unsubstantial lunch: the visit to museum and national library, [the bookhunt along Bedford row, Merchants Arch, Wellington Quay,] the music in the Ormond Hotel, the altercation in Bernard Kiernan's premises, a blank period of time including a cardrive, a visit to a house of mourning, a leavetaking, the eroticism produced by feminine exhibitionism, the prolonged delivery of Mrs Mina Purefoy, the visit to the ~~brothel~~ [disorderly house] of Mrs Bella Cohen, 82 Tyrone street, lower, and subsequent brawl in Beaver street, nocturnal perambulation to and from the cabman's shelter, Butt Bridge.

What imperfections in a perfect day did Bloom, walking, silently enumerate?
A ~~temporary~~ [provisional] failure to obtain renewal of an advertisement, to obtain a certain quantity of tea from Thomas Kernan (agent for Pullbrook, Robertson and Co., Mincing Lane, London, E. C.), to obtain admission (gratuitous or paid) to the performance of *Leah* by Mrs Bandman Palmer of the Gaiety Theatre, South Anne street.

What impression of an absent face did Bloom, arrested, silently recall?
The face of her father, the late Major Brian Cooper Tweedy, Royal Dublin Fusiliers, of Gibraltar and Rehoboth, Dolphin's Barn.

[Red star]
What personal objects were perceived by him?
A pair of new inodorous halfsilk black ladies' stockings, a pair of new violet garters, a pair of outsize ladies' drawers of India mull, cut on generous lines, redolent of opoponax, jessamine and Muratti's Turkish cigarettes and containing a long bright steel safety pin, folded curvilinear, a camisole of batiste with thin lace border, a short blue silk petticoat, all these objects being disposed irregularly on the top of a rectangular trunk, quadruple battened, [having capped corners,] with multicoloured labels, initialled on its fore side in white lettering B. C. T. (Brian Cooper Tweedy).

What impersonal objects were perceived?
Orangekeyed ware, bought of Henry Price, basket, fancy goods, chinaware and iron-mongery manufacturer, 21 to 23 Moore street, disposed irregularly on the washstand [and floor] and consisting of basin, soapdish and brushtray (on the washstand [together]), pitcher and night article (on the floor, separate)

[Red star]
Bloom's acts?
He deposited the articles of clothing on a chair, removed his other articles of clothing, took from beneath the bolster at the head of the bed a folded long white nightshirt, inserted his head and arms into the proper apertures of the nightshirt, removed a pillow from the head to the foot of the bed, prepared the bedlinen accordingly and entered the bed.

How?

With circumspection, as invariably when entering an abode (his own or not his own): with solicitude, the snakespiral springs of the mattress being old, the brass quoits and pendent viper radii loose and tremulous [under stress and strain]: prudently, as entering a lair or ambush of lust or adders: lightly, the less to disturb: reverently, the bed of conception and of birth ~~and dea~~, of consummation of marriage and of breach of marriage, of sleep, of death.

[Red star]

What did his limbs, when gradually extended, encounter?

New clean bedlinen, ~~the presence of~~ additional odours, the presence of a human form, female, hers, the imprint of a human form, male, not his, some crumbs, some flakes of potted meat, recooked, which he removed.

If he had smiled why would he have smiled?

To reflect that each one who enters imagines himself to be the first to enter whereas he is always the last term of a preceding series even if the first term of a succeeding one [, each imagining himself to be the first, last, only and alone, whereas he is neither first nor last nor only nor alone.]

What preceding series?

Assuming Mulvey to be the first term of his series, Penrose, Bartell d'Arcy, professor Goodwin, Julius Mastiansky, John Henry Menton, Father Bernard Corrigan, a farmer at the Royal Dublin Society's Horse Show, Maggot O'Reilly, Matthew Dillon, Valentine Blake Dillon (Lord Mayor of Dublin), Christopher Callinan, Lenehan, an Italian organgrinder, an unknown gentleman in the Gaiety Theatre, Benjamin Dollard, Simon Dedalus, Andrew (Pisser) Burke, Joseph Cuffe, Wisdom Hely, Alderman John Hooper, Dr Brady, Father Sebastian of Mount Argus, a bootblack at the General Post Office, Edward (Blazes) Boylan.

What were his reflections concerning the last member of this series and last occupant of the bed?

Reflections on his vigour [(a bounder)], corporal proportion [(a billsticker)], business ability [(a bester)], impressionability [(a boaster)].

Why this last quality?

Because he had observed [with augmenting frequency] in the preceding members of the same series the same concupiscence, inflammably transmitted, first with alarm, then with understanding, then with desire, finally with fatigue, with alternating symptoms of comprehension and apprehension.

[Red star]

With what [antagonistic] sentiments were his subsequent reflections affected?

Envy, jealousy, abnegation, equanimity.

[Red star]

Envy?

Of a bodily and mental [male] organism specially adapted for the superincumbent posture of energetic human copulation necessary for the complete satisfaction of a constant but not acute concupiscence resident in a bodily and mental female organism passive but not obtuse.

[Red star]

Jealousy?

Because a nature full and volatile, in her free state, was alternately the ~~source~~ agent and reagent of attraction. Because action between agents and reagents at all instants varied, with inverse proportion of increase and decrease, with ~~invariable~~ [incessant] circular extension and radial reentrance. Because the controlled contemplation of the fluctuation of attraction produced, if desired, a fluctuation of pleasure.

Abnegation?

In virtue of a) acquaintance initiated in September 1903 in the establishment of George Mesias, merchant tailor and outfitter, 5 Eden Quay, b) hospitality extended and received, c) comparative youth subject to influences of ambition and magnanimity.

Equanimity?

As not as calamitous as a cataclysmic annihilation of the planet in consequence of collision with a dark sun. As less reprehensible than theft, highway robbery, cruelty to children and animals, obtaining money under false pretenses, forgery, embezzlement, misappropriation of public money, betrayal of public trust, malingering, mayhem, corruption of minors, criminal libel, blackmail, contempt of court, arson, treason, felony, mutiny on the high seas, trespass, burglary, jailbreaking, practice of unnatural vice, desertion from armed forces in the field, perjury, poaching, usury, intelligence with the king's enemies, impersonation, criminal assault, manslaughter, wilful and premeditated murder. As not more abnormal than all other parallel processes of adaptation to altered conditions of existence, resulting in a reciprocal equilibrium between the bodily organism and its ~~eternal~~ [attendant] circumstances, foods, beverages, acquired habits, indulged inclinations, significant disease. As more than inevitable, irreparable.

What retribution, if any?

Assassination, never. Duel by combat, no. Divorce, not yet. Damages [by legal influence], not impossibly. Hushmoney [by moral influence], possibly. If any, positively, connivance, introduction of emulation, depreciation, alienation, humiliation, separation protecting the one separated from the other, protecting separator from both.

[Red star]

In what final satisfaction did these antagonistic sentiments and reflections converge?

Satisfaction at the ubiquity in eastern and western [terrestrial] hemispheres, of adipose [anterior and posterior] female hemispheres, redolent of excretory sanguine and seminal ~~animal~~ warmth, expressive of mute immutable mature animality.

[Red star]

The visible signs of antesatisfaction?

An approximate erection: a solicitous adversion: a gradual elevation: a tentative revelation: a silent contemplation.

[Red star]

Then?

He kissed the plump mellow yellow smellow melons of her rump, on each plump [melonous] hemisphere, in their mellow [yellow] furrow, with obscure prolonged provocative melonsmellonous osculation.

[Red star]   post

The visible signs of resatisfaction?
A silent contemplation: a tentative velation: a gradual abasement: a solicitous aversion: a proximate erection.

[Red star]
What followed this silent action?
Somnolent invocation, less somnolent recognition, incipient excitation, catechetical interrogation.

Did he With what modifications did the narrator reply to this interrogation?
Negative: he omitted to mention the [clandestine] correspondence between Martha Clifford and Henry Flower, the public altercation at, in and in the vicinity of the licensed premises of Bernard Kiernan and Co, Limited, 8, 9 and 10 Little Britain street, the erotic provocation and response thereto caused by the exhibitionism of Gertrude (Gerty), surname unknown. Positive: he included mention of a performance by Mrs. Bandman Palmer of *Leah* at the Gaiety Theatre, South Anne street, [a charitable visit to the National Lying-in Hotel Hospital, 29, 30 and 31 Holles Street,] an invitation to supper at Wynn's (Murphy's) Hotel, 35, 36 and 37 Lower Abbey street, a [temporary] concussion caused by a falsely calculated movement in the course of a postcenal gymnastic display, the victim (since completely recovered) being Stephen Dedalus, professor and author, eldest surviving son of Simon Dedalus, of no fixed occupation.

Was the narration otherwise unaltered by modifications?
Absolutely.

Which event or person emerged as the salient point of his narration?
Stephen Dedalus, professor and author.

What limitations of activity were perceived by listener and narrator concerning themselves during the course of this intermittent and increasingly laconic narration?
By the listener a limitation of fertility inasmuch as marriage have [*sic*] been celebrated one [2] calendar month[s] before [after] the 18th anniversary of her birth (8 September 1870), viz, 8 August [October], and consummated on the sam having-been-previously [and] consummated on the 10 July of the same year [same] with female issue born 15 June 1889, having been anticipatorily consummated on the 10 September of the same year and complete carnal intercourse, with ejaculation of semen with the [female] natural organ, having taken place 5 weeks previous, [viz, 27 November 1894,] to the birth [on 29 December 1894] of second (and only male) issue, deceased 9 January 1895, aged 11 days, there remained a period of 9 years, 5 months and 18 days during which carnal intercourse had been incomplete without ejaculation of semen within the natural female organ. By the narrator a limitation of activity, mental and corporal, inasmuch as complete mental intercourse [between himself and the listener] had not taken place since the consummation of puberty, indicated by catamenic hemorrhage, of the female issue of narrator and listener, 15 September 1903, there remained a period of 9 months and 1 day during which in consequence of a preestablished sexual [natural female] comprehension in incomprehension between the consummated females (listener and issue), complete corporal liberty of action had been inhibited. [circumscribed]

[Red star crossed out]
How?
By various reiterated interrogation concerning the place [destination] whither, the place

where, the time at which, the duration for which, the object with which in the case of temporary absences, projected or effected.

[Red star]
[What moved visibly above the listener's and the narrator's invisible thoughts?
The upcast reflection of a lamp and shade, an inconstant series of concentric circles of varying gradations of light and shadow.]

[Red star]
In what directions did listener and narrator lie?
Listener: S. E by E: Narrator N. W. by W: on the 53° of latitude, N and 6° of longitude, W: at an angle of 45° to the terrestrial equator.

[Red star]
In what state of rest or motion?
At rest relatively to themselves and to each other. In motion being each and both carried westward, forward and rereward respectively, by the proper perpetual motion of the earth through everchanging tracks of neverchanging space.

[Red star]
In what posture?
Listener: reclined semilaterally, left, left hand under head, right leg extended in a straight line and resting on left leg, flexed, in the attitude of Gea-Tellus, fulfilled, recumbent, big with seed. Narrator: reclined laterally, left, with right and left legs flexed, the [index and thumb of the] right hand resting on the bridge of the nose, in the attitude depicted in a shapshot photograph made by Percy Apjohn, the childman weary, the manchild in the womb.

[Red star]
Womb? Weary?
He rests. He has travelled.

[Red star]
With?
Sinbad the Sailor and Tinbad the Tailor and Jinbad the Jailer and Whinbad the Whaler and Ninbad the Nailer and Finbad the Failer and Binbad the Bailer and Pinbad the Pailer and Minbad the Mailer and Hinbad the Hailer and Rinbad the Railer and Dinbad the Kailer and Vinbad the Gailer and Linbad the Yailer and Xinbad the Phthailer.

[Red star]
When?
Going to [dark] bed there was a square round Sinbad the Sailor auk's rok's auk's egg in the [night of] bed of all the auks of the roks of the Darkinbad the Brightdayler.

Where?

•

(La réponse à la dernière demande est un point

Notes

Introduction and Chapter 1

1. A. Walton Litz, "Ithaca," in *James Joyce's "Ulysses": Critical Essays,* ed. Clive Hart and David Hayman (Berkeley: University of California Press, 1974), p. 386. This is the best analysis of Ithaca that I have seen.

2. Frank Budgen, *James Joyce and the Making of "Ulysses"* (1934; rpt. Bloomington: Indiana University Press, 1967), p. 258.

3. Ibid., p. 172.

4. Herbert Gorman quotes this material at length in *James Joyce*(New York: Rinehart, 1948), pp. 135–38.

5. Harry Levin, *James Joyce: A Critical Introduction* (1941; rpt. New York: New Directions, 1960), p. 95.

6. A number of these rough drafts for the episodes are missing. Some may quite possibly be extant, secluded in private hands. Neither Harriet Shaw Weaver nor Sylvia Beach, in letters to me, could offer assistance. Miss Beach surmised that "they disappeared in Joyce's removals from apartments and countries," and added, "It's surprising enough that anything exists of the *Ulysses* material, which spreads over seven years and many upheavals, not to mention Joyce's progressive eye trouble making it so difficult for him to keep his swirls of notes in any sort of order."

7. *Letters of James Joyce,* Vol. I, ed. Stuart Gilbert (New York: The Viking Press, 1957), p. 143.

8. Ibid., p. 150.

9. Ibid., p. 152.

10. Ibid., p. 161 (to Harriet Weaver).

11. *Letters of James Joyce,* Vol. III, ed. Richard Ellmann (New York: The Viking Press, 1966), p. 43.

12. Ibid., p. 46.

13. *Letters,* I:168 (to Harriet Weaver).

14. Ibid., p. 173.

15. Ibid. The first batch of Ithaca typescript runs to ten pages and covers the first eleven pages of the episode in the Modern Library edition, excluding, of course, many additions made later.

16. Ibid., p. 175.

17. Ibid.

18. Ibid., pp. 178–79.

19. *Letters,* III:57.

Chapter 2

1. Phillip F. Herring, ed., *Joyce's "Ulysses" Notesheets in the British Museum* (Charlottesville: The University Press of Virginia, 1972) and *Joyce's Notes and Early Drafts for "Ulysses": Selections from the Buffalo Collection* (Charlottesville, The University Press of Virginia, 1977). I am indebted to Professor Herring for confirming or correcting some of my uncertain readings among these notes.

2. *The James Joyce Archive,* Vol. 12, "ULYSSES: Notes & 'Telemachus'—'Scylla and Charybdis.' A Facsimile of Notes for the Book & Manuscripts & Typescripts for 1–9," (New York: Garland Publishing, Inc., 1977).

3. *James Joyce and the Making of "Ulysses,"* p. 173.

4. Sylvia Beach, *Shakespeare and Company* (New York: Harcourt, Brace and Company, 1959), p. 65. Joyce was writing the Circe episode at the time.

5. The original manuscript of this music is among the Buffalo typescripts. Joyce pasted the music on the typed page with the notation, "La musique est à photographier."

6. These notes were first described by A. Walton Litz in an important article, "Joyce's Notes for the Last Episodes of 'Ulysses,' " *Modern Fiction Studies* 4 (Spring 1958): 3–20. Phillip F. Herring, in his complete transcription of the notes in *Joyce's "Ulysses" Notesheets in the British Museum,* cited earlier, locates the application of each note, wherever possible, in the novel by page and line number.

7. Phillip Herring agrees with this estimate. *Joyce's "Ulysses" Notesheets in the British Museum,* p. 256.

8. John J. Slocum and Herbert Cahoon, in *A Bibliography of James Joyce* (New Haven: Yale University Press, 1953), item E.5.b.i., p. 140, state that the notebook contains "Manuscript notes for the following episodes, in order: Eumaeus, Circe, Nausicaa, Wandering Rocks, Hades, Oxen of the Sun, Cyclops, Ithaca, and Scylla and Charybdis." Actually this order is not correct; the episodes in the notebook are jumbled, with notes for some episodes appearing in more than one place. Slocum and Cahoon also omit Penelope, which is strongly represented.

9. Wyndham Lewis, *Time and Western Man* (London: Chatto & Windus, 1927), p. 107.

10. *Letters,* I:177.

11. Again, Phillip Herring agrees. *Joyce's Notes and Early Drafts for "Ulysses": Selections from the Buffalo Collection,* pp. 39–41.

12. Richard Ellmann, *James Joyce* (1959; new and rev. ed. New York: Oxford University Press, 1982), p. 671.

13. Thomas E. Connolly, ed., *James Joyce's Scribbledehobble: The Ur-Workbook for "Finnegans Wake"* (Evanston: Northwestern University Press, 1961).

14. A. Walton Litz, *James Joyce* (1966; rev. edn. Boston: Twayne Publishers, 1972), p. 118.

15. *Letters,* I: 172.

16. Valery Larbaud. "The *Ulysses* of James Joyce," *Criterion* I (October 1922):102. Larbaud's "underlined" here should be understood as meaning "crossed out" or "slashed through."

17. *Shakespeare and Company,* p. 65.

18. That colors have nothing to do with distinguishing episodes is strikingly illustrated by two entries in the Ithaca notesheets. "Never see dead donkey" and "(R.B.) shame of death" appear side by side on one sheet ("R.B." is Bloom's suicidal father, Rudolph). They are used, still side by side, in the Hades episode, as Bloom muses in the cemetery: "Far away a donkey brayed. Rain. No such ass. Never see a dead one, they say. Shame of death. They hide. Also poor papa went away." (110) Yet in the notesheets the first entry is cancelled in red, the second in blue.

19. A Walton Litz, *The Art of James Joyce: Method and Design in "Ulysses" and "Finnegans Wake"* (London: Oxford University Press, 1961), p. 20.

20. As seen earlier, the so-called "Ithaca" notes in the *Scribbledehobble* notebook contain many big words—probably because Joyce saw in them potentials for the linguistic miscegenations of *Finnegans Wake.*

21. *Letters,* I:178.

22. *Joyce's Notes and Early Drafts for "Ulysses": Selections from the Buffalo Collection,* pp. 49–50.

23. Thornton Wilder, "Joyce and the Modern Novel," in *A James Joyce Miscellany,* ed. Marvin Magalaner (New York: The James Joyce Society, 1957), p. 12.

24. As in the quoted entry, "LB etwas in cipher," Joyce often lapsed into foreign words for convenience and speed, thus lending many notes a *lingua franca* appearance. Most of these foreign intrusions, as one would expect, are Italian, and produce entries like "Suicide che ora?" (*Ulysses:* "Rudolph Bloom (Rudolph Virag) died...at some hour unstated" [684]), "geology embedded storia" (*Ulysses:* "the eons of geological periods recorded in the stratifications of the earth" [699]), and "laid out (spese)" (not used in book). Similar to this is Joyce's free use throughout the notes of words which so offended censors in the book itself. The following are typical:
     Woman's arse honest
     Star piss designs
     SD - Virtue is shite
     in darkest Africa (cunt)
     fuck creates love

25. *The Art of James Joyce,* p. 21.

Chapter 3

1. *James Joyce,* p. 513. With Ithaca, working against time, Joyce settled for three, not five, sets of proofs.

2. *Shakespeare and Company,* p. 58. As Joyce's publisher who saw many of the proofs

through the press, Miss Beach should have questioned his figure here. With Ithaca, for example, 15 percent was written on the proofs. Joyce was fond of making impressive claims about his labors, and rarely let the truth interfere with such opportunities. He loved to keen that he had spent one thousand hours writing Oxen of the Sun, or had completely rewritten Circe six, seven, or nine times, according to whichever version one reads.

3. *James Joyce and the Making of "Ulysses,"* p. 171.

4. *Letters,* I:156.

5. This entire manuscript has been published: *"Ulysses: A Facsimile of the Manuscript.* 3 vols. (Philadelphia: the Philip H. and A. S. W. Rosenbach Foundation, 1975).

6. *A Bibliography of James Joyce,* item E.5.g., p. 143. In the Pierpont Morgan Library, Herbert Cahoon showed me an early edition of *Ulysses* which included a single page of Ithaca typescript with Joyce's autograph additions (the page includes material from pp. 677, 678, and 679 of the Modern Library edition).

7. Described in detail by Peter Spielberg, *James Joyce's Manuscripts and Letters at the University of Buffalo: A Catalogue* (Buffalo: University of Buffalo, 1962), and published in *The James Joyce Archive,* Vol. 16, "ULYSSES: 'Ithaca' & 'Penelope.' A Facsimile of Manuscripts & Typescripts for Episodes 17 & 18," (New York: Garland Publishing, Inc., 1977).

8. Published in *The James Joyce Archive,* Vol. 21, "ULYSSES: 'Ithaca' & 'Penelope.' A Facsimile of Placards for Episodes 17–18," (New York: Garland Publishing, Inc., 1977).

9. Published in *The James Joyce Archive,* Vol. 27, "ULYSSES: 'Eumaeus,' 'Ithaca,' & 'Penelope.' A facsimile of Page Proofs for Episodes 16–18," (New York: Garland Publishing, Inc., 1977).

10. In one change, Joyce failed to achieve complete accuracy. He changed the census of 1901 from 4,235,000 to 4,386,035 (718), but the official count for 1901 was 4,458,775. Only Joyce's painstaking care with such details makes so trivial an error worth noting.

11. Bloom's soap raises another problem. Several commentators have noted that it was bought not thirteen hours previously, as the text states, but sixteen hours. Thirteen appears in manuscript and survives six drafts to become inalterably enshrined in the final text. Some critics propose that the error is not Joyce's but Bloom's, and since Joyce actually caught another error in the same line (the soap's cost), it seems unlikely he would miss this one. On the other hand, the cost error involved only an inconsistency between "four" in one place and "three" in another, and could easily be spotted, whereas the time error involved a calculation of hours which, once made, however incorrectly, would probably not be rechecked. Perhaps the best attitude to take is that of James Thurber toward a mystifying but trivial incident recalled from his youth: "I don't think about it much anymore."

12. Similar to these lapses, though not actually an error or contradiction, is the matter of Bloom's cat, which leaves the house while the two men talk in the kitchen and returns when Bloom leads Stephen out the back door. If we never learn where Stephen spends this night, at least the cat's accommodation is finally assured, however tardily. Joyce lets the cat out in the manuscript, but either forgets or does not decide to let her back in until the final proof, where he adds the permissive question.

13. Ellmann, *James Joyce,* p. 514.

14. *Letters,* I:176 (to Harriet Weaver).

15. Ibid., I:183 (to Harriet Weaver).

16. For the further adventures of this word after publication, see Grover Smith, Jr., "The Cryptogram in Joyce's *Ulysses:* A Misprint," *Publications of the Modern Language Association* LXXIII (September, 1958):446–47.

Chapter 4

1. *Letters,* I:175.

2. William Empson, "The Theme of *Ulysses,*" *Kenyon Review* XVIII (Winter, 1956):34.

3. Edmund Wilson, *Axel's Castle* (New York: Charles Scribner's Sons, 1931), p. 216.

4. *James Joyce: A Critical Introduction,* p. 120.

5. David Daiches, *The Novel and the Modern World* (1939; rev. ed. Chicago: University of Chicago Press, 1960), p. 144.

6. Richard Ellmann, *Ulysses on the Liffey* (New York: Oxford University Press, 1972), p. 158.

7. Philip Toynbee, in Seon Givens, ed., *James Joyce: Two Decades of Criticism* (1948; rpt. New York: Vanguard Press, 1963), p. 281.

8. Joseph Prescott, "James Joyce: A Study in Words," *Publications of the Modern Language Association* LIV (March 1939):313.

9. "Ithaca," in *James Joyce's "Ulysses": Critical Essays,* p. 392.

10. Marilyn French, *The Book as World: James Joyce's "Ulysses"* (Cambridge, Mass.: Harvard University Press, 1976), pp. 220, 222.

11. Ibid., p. 221.

12. Rebecca West sounded an early *cave canem* by lamenting that Joyce's "technique is a tin can tied to the tail of the dog of his genius." *The Strange Necessity* (Garden City, N.Y.: Doubleday, Doran and Co., 1928), p. 52.

13. Letter to Joyce, *Letters,* III:58.

14. Gorman, *James Joyce,* pp. 98–99.

15. Besides such a bone-marrow influence as Aquinas, Joyce was more immediately drawn to the interrogative method by the specific example of its simplistic use in Richmal Mangnall's *Historical and Miscellaneous Questions for the Use of Young People, with a Selection of British and General Biography,* 1862. See R. A. Copland and G. W. Turner, "The Nature of James Joyce's Parody in 'Ithaca'," *Modern Language Review* 64 (October 1969):759–63.

16. Hugh Kenner, *Dublin's Joyce* (Bloomington: Indiana University Press, 1956), p. 241.

17. *Letters,* I:164 (to Claud W. Sykes) and I:159 (to Frank Budgen).

18. *Time and Western Man,* pp. 107, 108.

19. Gustave Flaubert, *Madame Bovary,* trans. E. M. Aveling, ed. Charles I. Weir, Jr. (New York: A. A. Knopf, 1948), pp. 2, 31.

20. Ibid., p. 82.

21. *The Novel and the Modern World,* p. 144.

22. *Time and Western Man,* p. 107.

23. John Greenway, " A Guide through James Joyce's *Ulysses,*" *College English* 17 (November 1955):77.

24. *The Novel and the Modern World,* p. 146.

25. *Letters,* I:159–60 (to Frank Budgen).

26. William York Tindall, *James Joyce: His Way of Interpreting the Modern World* (New York: Charles Scribner's Sons, 1950), p. 91, and Kenner, *Dublin's Joyce,* p. 261.

27. *James Joyce and the Making of "Ulysses,"* pp. 257–58.

28. *The Novel and the Modern World,* p. 81.

29. I am indebted to Professor Gilbert Highet for suggesting this point about Ithaca's objective style.

30. *James Joyce and the Making of "Ulysses,"* p. 188.

31. *James Joyce: A Critical Introduction,* p. 121.

Chapter 5

1. J. I. M. Stewart, *James Joyce* (London: Longmans, Green & Co., 1957), p. 31.

2. "James Joyce: *Ulysses,*" *Invitation to Learning* 2 (Spring 1952):69.

3. *James Joyce: A Critical Introduction,* pp. 70, 120–21, 133.

4. David Daiches, *The Present Age in British Literature* (Bloomington: Indiana University Press, 1958), pp. 96–97.

5. *The Art of James Joyce,* p. 22.

6. *James Joyce and the Making of "Ulysses,"* p. 57.

Chapter 6

1. Several page-by-page commentaries on all the episodes have been published, such as William York Tindall, *A Reader's Guide to James Joyce* (New York: Farrar, Straus & Giroux, 1959), Weldon Thornton, *Allusions in "Ulysses": An Annotated List* (Chapel Hill: The University of North Carolina Press, 1968), and particularly Don Gifford and Robert J. Seidman, *Notes for Joyce: An Annotation of James Joyce's "Ulysses"* (New York: E. P. Dutton, 1974). The glossary here may duplicate or differ with some points in these books; the interested reader is referred to them for additional or more detailed information.

2. Considering Joyce's practice in other episodes, one might expect to find Ithaca packed with ingenious references to bones, but the episode is extraordinarily boneless. *Ulysses*

contains 5 mentions of "skeleton," 34 of "bone," 20 of "skull," 15 of "jaw," 11 of "rib," to sample just a few possibilities, and not one of these occurs in Ithaca.

3. Joseph Prescott, "Leopold Bloom's Memory Concerning Cormac's Death," *Notes and Queries* CXCVI (1951):434.

4. *James Joyce*, p. 290.

5. Robert M. Adams, *Surface and Symbol: The Consistency of James Joyce's "Ulysses"* (New York: Oxford University Press, 1962), p. 226.

6. Letter to me from Dr. R. J. Hayes, Director, National Library of Ireland.

7. Hugh Kenner, *"Ulysses"* (London: George Allen & Unwin, 1980), p. 136.

8. Adams, *Surface and Symbol,* p. 78. For additional information see Thornton, *Allusions in "Ulysses,"* p. 464.

9. *James Joyce*, p. 371.

10. *James Joyce and the Making of "Ulysses"*, p. 186.

11. *Allusions in "Ulysses,"* p. 469, and *Notes for Joyce*, p. 474.

12. *Surface and Symbol*, p. 138.

13. Vladimir Nabokov, *Lectures on Literature* (New York: Harcourt Brace Jovanovich, 1980), p. 359.

14. Francis James Child, *The English and Scottish Popular Ballads* (New York: Little, Brown and Company, 1882–1898), III:251.

15. William Wells Newell, *Games and Songs of American Children* (New York: Harper & Brothers, 1883), p. 75.

16. Ellmann, *James Joyce*, p. 521. Jacques Benoîst-Méchin also translated parts of *Ulysses* for Valery Larbaud's prepublication lecture.

17. "The Theme of *Ulysses*," p. 35.

18. *A Reader's Guide to James Joyce*, p. 229.

19. *Letters*, I:129 (to Harriet Weaver).

20. *Ulysses on the Liffey*, p. 156.

21. Hugh Kenner, "Molly's Masterstroke," *James Joyce Quarterly* 10 (Fall 1972):19–28.

22. Margaret Honton, "Molly's Mistresstroke," *James Joyce Quarterly* 14 (Fall 1976):25–29.

23. *Lectures on Literature*, p. 360.

24. *Letters*, I:177.

25. Thomas E. Connolly, *The Personal Library of James Joyce: A Descriptive Bibliography* (Buffalo: University of Buffalo Bookstore, 1957), p. 33.

26. *James Joyce*, following p. 184.

27. "Molly's Masterstroke," p. 23.

28. *Letters*, I:177.

29. *"Ulysses,"* p. 143.

30. *The Book as World,* p. 234.

31. "The Cryptogram in Joyce's *Ulysses:* A Misprint," p. 446.

32. *Surface and Symbol,* p. 184.

33. *"Ulysses,"* p. 165.

34. Zack Bowen, *Musical Allusions in the Works of James Joyce* (Albany: State University of New York Press, 1974), p. 329.

37. Ellmann, *James Joyce,* p. 464.

38. Edmund Epstein, "Cruxes in *Ulysses,*" *The James Joyce Review* I (September 15, 1957):31.

39. Aldous Huxley and Stuart Gilbert, *Joyce the Artificer: Two Studies of Joyce's Method* (London: privately printed, 1952), p. [7].

40. *James Joyce,* p. 516.

41. As the Blooms, so the Joyces: a letter to Stanislaus Joyce confides, "Our room is quite small: one bed: we sleep 'lying opposed in opposite directions, the head of one towards the tail of the other.' " *Letters,* II:202.

40. Herbert Howarth, "The Joycean Comedy: Wilde, Jonson, and Others," in *A James Joyce Miscellany,* Second Series, ed. Marvin Magalaner (Carbondale: Southern Illinois University Press, 1959), pp. 179–80.

41. *The Strange Necessity,* p. 14.

42. Erwin R. Steinberg, "A Book with a Molly in It," *The James Joyce Review* 2 (Autumn 1958):56.

43. J. Mitchell Morse, "Molly Bloom Revisited," in *A James Joyce Miscellany,* Second Series, pp. 148–49.

44. *James Joyce,* p. 118.

45. *James Joyce,* pp. 23–24.

Bibliography

Adams, Robert M. *James Joyce: Common Sense and Beyond*. New York: Random House, 1966.
——————. *Surface and Symbol: The Consistency of James Joyce's "Ulysses."* New York: Oxford University Press, 1962.

Beach, Sylvia. *Shakespeare and Company*. New York: Harcourt, Brace and Company, 1959.

Bowen, Zack. *Musical Allusions in the Works of James Joyce: Early Poetry through "Ulysses."* New York: State University of New York Press, 1974.

Budgen, Frank. *James Joyce and the Making of "Ulysses."* 1934; rpt. Bloomington: Indiana University Press, 1967.

Burgess, Anthony. *Joysprick: An Introduction to the Language of James Joyce*. London: Andre Deutsch Limited, 1973.
——————. *ReJoyce*. New York: Ballantine Books, 1966.

Child, Francis James. *The English and Scottish Popular Ballads*. New York: Little, Brown and Company, 1882–1898.

Connolly, Thomas E. *James Joyce's Scribbledehobble: The Ur-Workbook for "Finnegans Wake."* Evanston, Illinois: Northwestern University Press, 1961.
——————. *The Personal Library of James Joyce: A Descriptive Bibliography*. Buffalo: University of Buffalo Bookstore, 1957.

Copland, R. A., and G. W. Turner. "The Nature of James Joyce's Parody in 'Ithaca'." *Modern Language Review* 64 (October 1969): 759–63.

Daiches, David. *The Novel and the Modern World*. 1939; rev. ed. Chicago: University of Chicago Press, 1960.
——————. *The Present Age in British Literature*. Bloomington: Indiana University Press, 1958.

Damon, S. Foster. "The Odyssey in Dublin." In *James Joyce: Two Decades of Criticism*. Ed. Seon Givens. New York: Vanguard Press, 1948.

Eliot, T. S. "*Ulysses*, Order and Myth." In *James Joyce: Two Decades of Criticism*. Ed. Seon Givens. New York: Vanguard Press, 1948.

Ellmann, Richard. *The Consciousness of Joyce*. New York: Oxford University Press, 1977.
——————. *James Joyce*. 1959; new and rev. ed. New York: Oxford University Press, 1982.
——————. *Ulysses on the Liffey*. New York: Oxford University Press, 1972.

Empson, William. "The Theme of *Ulysses*." *Kenyon Review* XVIII (Winter 1956):26–52.

Epstein, Edmund. "Cruxes in *Ulysses*." *The James Joyce Review* I (September 15, 1957): 25–36.

Finneran, Richard J., ed. *Anglo-Irish Literature: A Review of Research*. New York: The Modern Language Association of America, 1976.

Flaubert, Gustave. *Madame Bovary*. Translated by E. M. Aveling. New York: A. A. Knopf, 1948.

Fleishman, Avrom. "Science in Ithaca." *Contemporary Literature* VIII (Summer 1967): 377–91.

French, Marilyn. *The Book as World: James Joyce's "Ulysses."* Cambridge, Mass.: Harvard University Press, 1976.

Gifford, Don, and Robert J. Seidman. *Notes for Joyce: An Annotation of James Joyce's "Ulysses."* New York: E. P. Dutton, 1974.

Gilbert, Stuart. *James Joyce's "Ulysses," A Study*. 1930; rpt. New York: Random House, 1952.

Givens, Seon, ed. *James Joyce: Two Decades of Criticism*. 1948; rpt. New York: Vanguard Press, 1963.

Goldberg, S. L. *The Classical Temper: A Study of James Joyce's "Ulysses."* New York: Barnes & Noble, 1961.

Goodwin, Murray. "Three Wrong Turns in *Ulysses*." *Western Review* 15 (1951):223–24.

Gorman, Herbert. *James Joyce*. New York: Rinehart & Company, 1948.

Greenway, John. "A Guide through James Joyce's *Ulysses*." *College English* 17 (November 1955):67–78.

Hanley, Miles. *A Word Index to James Joyce's "Ulysses."* Madison: University of Wisconsin Press, 1951.

Hart, Clive, *James Joyce's "Ulysses."* Adelaide, Australia: Sydney University Press, 1968.

—————, and David Hayman, eds. *James Joyce's "Ulysses": Critical Essays*. Berkeley: University of California Press, 1974.

Hayman, David. *The Mechanics of Meaning*. Englewood Cliffs, N.J.: Prentice-Hall, 1970.

Herring, Phillip F., ed. *Joyce's Notes and Early Drafts for "Ulysses": Selections from the Buffalo Collection*. Charlottesville: The University Press of Virginia, 1977.

—————. *Joyce's "Ulysses" Notesheets in the British Museum*. Charlottesville: The University Press of Virginia, 1972.

Honton, Margaret. "Molly's Mistresstroke." *James Joyce Quarterly* 14 (Fall 1976):25–29.

Huxley, Aldous, and Stuart Gilbert. *Joyce the Artificer: Two Studies of Joyce's Method*. London: privately printed, 1952.

"James Joyce: *Ulysses*." *Invitation to Learning* 2 (Spring 1952):63–70.

Joyce, James. *The James Joyce Archive*. Vol. 12. "ULYSSES: Notes & 'Telemachus'— 'Scylla and Charybdis.' A Facsimile of Notes for the Book & Manuscripts & Typescripts for Episodes 1–9." New York: Garland Publishing, Inc., 1977.

—————. *The James Joyce Archive*. Vol. 16. "ULYSSES: 'Ithaca' & 'Penelope.' A Facsimile of Manuscripts & Typescripts for Episodes 17 & 18." New York: Garland Publishing, Inc., 1977.

—————. *The James Joyce Archive*. Vol. 21. "ULYSSES: 'Ithaca' & 'Penelope.' A Facsimile of Placards for Episdoes 17–18." New York: Garland Publishing, Inc., 1977.

—————. *The James Joyce Archive*. Vol. 27. "ULYSSES: 'Eumaeus,' 'Ithaca,' & 'Penelope.' A Facsimile of Page Proofs for Episodes 16–18." New York: Garland Publishing, Inc., 1977.

—————. *Letters of James Joyce*. Vol. I. Ed. Stuart Gilbert, 1957; rev. Richard Ellmann, 1966. New York: The Viking Press, 1966. Vols. II and III. Ed. Richard Ellmann. New York: The Viking Press, 1966.

—————. *A Portrait of the Artist as a Young Man*. 1964; corrected text New York: The Viking Press, 1972.

—————. *Selected Joyce Letters*. Ed. Richard Ellmann. New York: The Viking Press, 1975.

—————. *Ulysses*. Paris: Shakespeare and Company, 1922.

—————. *Ulysses*. 8th printing. Paris: Shakespeare and Company, 1926.

—————. *Ulysses*. Hamburg: Odyssey Press, 1932.

—————. *Ulysses*. 1934: corrected and reset New York: The Modern Library, 1961.

—————. *Ulysses: A Facsimile of the Manuscript*. 3 vols. Philadelphia: the Philip H. and A. S. W. Rosenbach Foundation, 1975.

Kain, Richard M. *Fabulous Voyager: James Joyce's "Ulysses."* 1947; rpt. New York: The Viking Press, 1966.

Kenner, Hugh. *Dublin's Joyce*. Bloomington: Indiana University Press, 1956.

—————. *Joyce's Voices*. Berkeley: University of California Press, 1978.

—————. "Molly's Masterstroke." *James Joyce Quarterly* 10 (Fall 1972):19-28.

—————. *"Ulysses."* London: George Allen & Unwin, 1980.

Knight, Douglas. "The Reading of *Ulysses*." *ELH: A Journal of English Literary History* 19 (1952):64-80.

Larbaud, Valery. "The *Ulysses* of James Joyce." *Criterion* I (October 1922):94-10.

Lawrence, Karen. *The Odyssey of Style in "Ulysses."* Princeton: Princeton University Press, 1981.

Levin, Harry. *James Joyce: A Critical Introduction*. 1941; rpt. New York: New Directions Books, 1960.

Lewis, Wyndham. *Time and Western Man*. London: Chatto & Windus, 1927.

Lidderdale, Jane, and Mary Nicholson. *Dear Miss Weaver: Harriet Shaw Weaver 1876-1961*. New York: The Viking Press, 1970.

Litz, A. Walton. *The Art of James Joyce: Method and Design in "Ulysses" and "Finnegans Wake."* London: Oxford University Press, 1961.

—————. *James Joyce*. 1966; rev. edn. Boston: Twayne Publishers, 1972.

—————. "Joyce's Notes for the Last Episodes of 'Ulysses'." *Modern Fiction Studies* 4 (Spring 1958):3-20.

Madtes, Richard E. "Joyce and the Building of Ithaca." *ELH: A Journal of English Literary History* 31 (December 1964):443-59.

Magalaner, Marvin, ed. *A James Joyce Miscellany*. New York: The James Joyce Society, 1957.

—————. *A James Joyce Miscellany*. Second Series. Carbondale: Southern Illinois University Press, 1959.

—————. *A James Joyce Miscellany*. Third Series. Carbondale: Southern Illinois University Press, 1962.

—————, and Richard M. Kain. *Joyce: The Man, the Work, and the Reputation*. 1956; rpt. New York: Collier Books, 1962.

Marre, K. E. "Experimentation with a Symbol from Mythology: The Courses of the Comets in the 'Ithaca' Chapter of Ulysses." *Modern Fiction Studies* 20 (Autumn 1974):385-90.

Nabokov, Vladimir. *Lectures on Literature*. New York: Harcourt Brace Jovanovich, 1980.

Newell, William Wells. *Games and Songs of American Children*. New York; Harper & Brothers, 1883.

O'Brien, Darcy. *The Conscience of James Joyce*. Princeton: Princeton University Press, 1968.

Peake, C. H. *James Joyce: The Citizen and the Artist*. Stanford, California: Stanford University Press, 1977.

Prescott, Joseph. *Exploring James Joyce*. Carbondale: Southern Illinois University Press, 1964.

—————. "Leopold Bloom's Memory Concerning Cormac's Death." *Notes and Queries* CXCVI (1951):434.

—————. "James Joyce: A Study in Words." *Publications of the Modern Language Association* LIV (March 1939):304–15.

Raleigh, John Henry. "Who was M'Intosh?" *The James Joyce Review* 3 (1959):59–62.

Russell, Bertrand. *Introduction to Mathematical Philosophy.* London: George Allen & Unwin, 1919.

Schutte, William M. *Joyce and Shakespeare: A Study in the Meaning of "Ulysses."* New Haven: Yale University, 1957.

————— and Erwin R. Steinberg. "The Fictional Technique of *Ulysses.*" In *Approaches to "Ulysses": Ten Essays.* Ed. Thomas F. Staley and Bernard Benstock. Pittsburgh: University of Pittsburgh Press, 1970.

Seidel, Michael. *Epic Geography: James Joyce's "Ulysses."* Princeton: Princeton University Press, 1976.

Slocum, John J., and Herbert Cahoon. *A Bibliography of James Joyce.* New Haven: Yale University Press, 1953.

Smith, Grover, Jr. "The Cryptogram in Joyce's *Ulysses:* A Misprint." *Publications of the Modern Language Association* LXXIII (September 1958):446–47.

Spielberg, Peter. *James Joyce's Manuscripts and Letters at the University of Buffalo: A Catalogue.* Buffalo: University of Buffalo, 1962.

Staley, Thomas F., ed. *"Ulysses": Fifty Years.* Bloomington: Indiana University Press, 1974.

————— and Bernard Benstock, ed. *Approaches to "Ulyssess": Ten Essays.* Pittsburgh: University of Pittsburgh Press, 1970.

Steinberg, Erwin R. "A Book with a Molly in It." *The James Joyce Review* 2 (Autumn 1958):55–62.

—————. *The Stream of Consciousness and Beyond in "Ulysses."* Pittsburgh: University of Pittsburgh Press, 1973.

Stewart, J. I. M. *James Joyce.* London: Longmans, Green & Co., 1957.

Sultan, Stanley. *The Argument of "Ulysses."* Columbus: Ohio State University Press, 1965.

Thornton, Weldon. *Allusions in "Ulysses": An Annotated List.* Chapel Hill: The University of North Carolina Press, 1968.

Tindall, William York. *Forces in Modern British Literature, 1885–1946.* New York: Alfred A. Knopf, 1949.

—————. *James Joyce: His Way of Interpreting the Modern World.* New York; Charles Scribner's Sons, 1950.

—————. *A Reader's Guide to James Joyce.* New York: Farrar, Straus & Giroux, 1959.

Toynbee, Philip. " A Study of James Joyce's *"Ulysses."* In *James Joyce: Two Decades of Criticism.* Ed. Seon Givens. New York: Vanguard Press, 1948.

Tracy, Robert. "Leopold Bloom Fourfold: A Hungarian-Hebraic-Hellenic-Hibernian Hero." *Massachusetts Review* 6 (Spring-Summer 1965):523–38.

West, Rebecca. *The Strange Necessity.* Garden City, N. Y.: Doubleday, Doran and Co., 1928.

Wilson, Edmund. *Axel's Castle.* New York: Charles Scribner's Sons, 1931.

Index